WITNESS

Voices and Choices

To Karen.
Enjoy ♡ C.

JIŘÍ (GEORGE) HOŘÁK

◆ FriesenPress

Suite 300 - 990 Fort St
Victoria, B C , V 8 V 3 K 2
Canada

www.friesenpress.com

ISBN
978-1-4602-9593-9 (Hardcover)
978-1-4602-9594-6 (Paperback)
978-1-4602-9595-3 (eBook)

1. RELIGION, CHRISTIAN LIFE, PERSONAL GROWTH

Distributed to the trade by The Ingram Book Company

Table of Contents

Acknowlegements

MY SINCERE THANKS GO TO MY FRIEND AND EDITOR Douglas Francis Mitchell. Without his prompting and help, this book would have never been written. Doug is a retired high school English teacher and principal, a musician and a writer. My thanks go also to Josef Svoboda, whose feedback on my draft has been quite helpful. The critical feedback of Father Jiří Macenauer of Burlington, Ontario, was also helpful.

My deep gratitude for the initial guidance on my earthly pilgrimage belongs to my mother and father. I became fully aware of their spiritual impact only after I grew up. It was their love, sacrifices, prayers, and living faith that supported me. Mr. František Javora, along with his family, had a significant influence on me during my youthful formation years.

The real opening of my full life-horizons, a kind of inner conversion and enlightenment, took place at a three day Ignatian retreat in Brno, directed by Father Nesrovnal, S.J, in the fall of 1947.

On the path that followed, my influential spiritual directors and guides were the late Bishop Felix Maria Davídek, Father David Asselin, S.J. of the English speaking Canadian Jesuit Province, and most of all the late

Cardinal Tomáš Špidlík, S.J., a theologian and author of many books and publications in many languages, Russian and Arabic included.

Vera, my Protestant wife, who eventually joined us Catholics, must be added to this short list. Her spirituality was real and deep, humble and modest, down-to-earth, yet intellectually sharp.

There are other people who walked shorter or longer distances with me on the path of life. To all of them, I am grateful for their goodness, their friendship, their understanding, their support, and most of all, their prayers.

Jiří (George) Hořák
Cranbrook, BC, Canada

Introduction

IN A WORLD PURSUING POWER, PLEASURE, FORTUNE and fame, George Horak was an anomaly. He was a humble mystic seeking truth in his life experiences and in his relationship with God.

I met George in the fall of 2010 when he asked me to drive him to Calgary for a doctor's appointment. After listening to his stories and appreciating his knowledge of history and his analytical perceptions of world events, I knew this man was unusual. I had many questions about his education, background, and experiences.

I suggested he share his experiences in writing so that others could benefit from his view of the world and his faith journey. George didn't think his life or opinions would be of interest to the public. Finally, he succumbed to my arguments that our world needs to hear stories like his faith-guided journey, and that he had a responsibility to contribute his knowledge and experience, since he had the benefit of good books. Although fluent in five languages, writing in English was not an easy task. When I agreed to help with editing, he agreed to begin writing.

He listened to the voice of God, listened to the voice of his conscience, made choices, and accepted the consequences without bitterness or regret. He remained a faithful witness throughout his eighty-seven-year journey. From his childhood in Czechoslovakia, his journey has taken him to Venezuela, Italy, Austria, United States and finally to Canada. He died on October 3, 2016 in Cranbrook, BC, shortly after completing edits for this book.

It has been a privilege to support my friend on his journey. I have been edified by his life and by his writing; I believe the reader also will be edified.

Douglas Francis Mitchell
Cranbrook, BC

I. CHILDHOOD AND TEENAGE YEARS

1. Family Background

MY FATHER'S ANCESTORS CAME TO THE POOR region of Valašsko in Moravia from northern Bohemia after the Thirty Years' Catholic-Protestant War in the early seventeenth century. My family's name, Hořák (hook over the r), supposedly was the name of a cannonier soldier responsible for the fire necessary for firing cannons.

Both my parents were orphans who did not experience a normal family life. From the little I know about my father's childhood, it was extremely harsh. Josef was born in 1897, the third of five children. They lived in the small mountain village of Nedašov in Moravia. When he was about seven years old, he lost his father in an accident. My grandmother remained alone, raising five children between the ages of one and eleven in extreme poverty.

My father did well in school. His teachers suggested that my grandmother send him for higher education to develop his talent for painting. His mother had no money, no insurance, and no support for her orphaned family. With hard work and her children's help, she kept a modest house, milked their cow, and worked their few stony fields. There was no electricity in the village, no church, and no conveniences except for a general store. At the age of fourteen, my father was sent from the small backward village with thatch roofs to the city of Brno to become a painter, ironically a house-painter. In this craft he became a professional journeyman and eventually opened his own business. As a teenager, he joined Sokol, a gymnastics organization with strong nationalistic and anti-Catholic tendencies. Later on as a young, self-confident adult, he was involved in politics. For a short time, he served as the youngest mayor of Nedašov. As mayor, he dealt with local injustices against the poor.

Some of the controversial local situations in Nedašov had to be decided in court. There he won a case and also lost one. He was frustrated with the case he lost and confronted the magistrate, openly criticizing his judgment in the courtroom. The magistrate sent him to jail for insulting the court. My father expected the people whom he had helped to stand by him, but they did not. He felt betrayed and abandoned by everybody, and eventually suffered an emotional breakdown. The jail superintendent, not knowing what to do with him, sent for his mother to take him home.

The day he returned from the hospital, my father's older sister Veronica prayed for him while he swore and kicked at a holy picture hanging on the wall. He recovered from his breakdown through a religious experience in which he had a vision of the compassionate presence of Christ in the form of the Sacred Heart of Jesus silently standing at his bed and looking at him with love. My father told me these things when I was a young teenager.

A certain amount of resentment, bitterness, and distrust towards political and legal systems remained in him for the rest of his life. The only people he trusted and honoured were Roman Catholic priests. They were his conservative advisers when he experienced difficulties in his own family life.

My parents married in June, 1928. My mother was six years younger than my father. I know almost nothing about my mother's childhood except that she lost both parents early in her life and grew up an orphan in the city of Brno. She mentioned how harsh it was for her during World War I when she and her friends suffered great hunger. She related how they would dig in the woods for roots and sometimes ate cornbread filled with sawdust.

I don't know when and where my parents met, except that it was during a Roman Catholic Marian pilgrimage. They were both prayerful people. As a child, I modelled myself after my mother, not my father. I had no desire to be as harsh and dominant as my father. In spite of his harsh bossiness and superiority, from time to time he showed his tender heart and playfulness.

Our family prayed every day and strictly observed Sundays and Christian feast days. We also followed the

Roman Catholic canon law on fasting and abstinence. Very rare exceptions were allowed. Because of the consistency in discipline and the authentic caring of both parents, particularly my mother, we children did not have serious emotional problems in spite of our poverty. We knew precisely what to expect and how to act. Our Christian neighbours, the Javoras and their ten children, shared their house with us and were a great support. We considered them our extended family.

2. Childhood

I WAS BORN IN 1929 IN A MATERNITY WARD IN BRNO, Moravia. One year after my birth, my parents settled with the Javoras family in the town of Chrlice, close to the industrial city of Brno. My memories go back to the earliest stages of my life in the form of pictures, something like snapshots or colour photographs. When I mentioned to my mother some of the events from the earliest days of my life, she wondered how I could know about them. She couldn't believe that it was possible for a baby to remember such things.

I clearly recall that the Javoras' new house had wooden steps to the attic. I remember that I couldn't walk yet, but I could move on my belly and later on all fours. I wasn't allowed near those steps that kept challenging my curiosity. One beautiful spring morning, my mother was busy in the kitchen. The door to the attic steps was open. I crawled towards the steps determined to climb them. I climbed up to the fifth step, and then panic hit me. How would I get back down? I knew how to move forwards, but not backwards. I managed to turn around and slide down on my belly, hitting each step with my head. I remember the stars in my head to this day.

I was also curious about what was on the kitchen table. I could only see it if my mother or father took me in their arms. One day I managed to get up from my crawling position by holding on to one of the table legs, grabbing the edge of the table and lifting myself so that my eyes were level with the surface of the table. There was nothing there. To this day I feel the satisfaction of finding out on my own that there was nothing on the table. There are other such memories from my early childhood, but these two incidents make my point.

When I was four, my brother Joe was born. My father's name was Josef, so the baby had to be named Josef. Normally as the first born I would have been baptized Josef, but I was born on the feast of St. George. My grandfather and great-grandfather were named George; therefore, I could not be named Josef. I became George (Jiří in Czech).

After Joe was born, he took my place as the focus of my parents' attention. I was told that I was a big boy and he was a baby. Little Joe wasn't stupid and soon discovered how to dominate me. When we'd play together, he would scream and cry. My father would come immediately and punish me, and Joe would stop crying and smile. When we were alone, I beat him until blood dripped from his nose.

I developed respect and admiration for Joe only when he became a teenager. I loved him and could count on him. When he was nineteen, he was sentenced by the communists to four years in prison for espionage. After three weeks in a solitary cell, he was sent to the uranium mines where young and old men worked under Soviet command. They were exposed to harmful radiation with no protective gear. When I met Joe again in 1990 after the Soviet Union collapsed and Czechoslovakia was liberated, I tried to apologize to him for my childhood cruelty. He didn't know what I was talking about.

My closest friend from my earliest years was Alois, one of the Javoras boys. We were like two inseparable brothers, always playing together, getting into mischief together, and receiving punishment together. This close relationship lasted until we were sixteen. It gradually fell apart, but it never died. Alois was excellent at throwing stones at targets like birds, public street lights or glass isolators on telephone poles. I never could manage as well as he did. He was musically talented, and I was not. Usually I suggested some prank that he executed.

Because of an injury I had suffered when I was ten, I limped and couldn't run as well as other boys, so I was often the goalie in soccer or handball games. In one handball match, I injured my right knee badly. The wound started to fester and the knee required surgery. I ended up in the hospital again, this time for two weeks. Now at my old age of eighty-four, I'm having trouble with the knee again. On top of that, I have arthritis in both legs and in my back.

When I was in grade one, I sensed a growing tension between my father and my mother. They were arguing in front of me. On one occasion, their argument went so far that my mother said, "Alright! I'm leaving you. You may keep Jiří and I will take little Joe. Goodbye!" I started to cry. How could she say such a thing? If my parents were separating, I wanted to go with her. Little Joe could go with my father. Seeing me crying, they stopped their argument. In September, 1936, my sister Margaret was born. There was no longer any talk about ending their marriage. I suspect that a priest's counselling had something to do with it.

I loved Margaret dearly and was proud of her. She was beautiful, gentle and smart. As a teenager, she was elected president of the student council.

3. Am I Clairvoyant?

I BELIEVE THAT EVERYONE HAS THE POTENTIAL TO be clairvoyant or intuitive, whatever term you prefer, provided that his/her intuition is not blocked by a rationalistic, critical attitude. Intuitive people are normal. With consistent experiences and a bit of education, they learn to trust their inner feelings and inspirations. This is particularly true of artists, saints and mystics.

When I was five years old, I had a vivid dream. I saw a clean, wooden box full of apples. When I awoke, I told my mother that our grandmother was sending us apples in a wooden box. My mother told me that was only a dream because our grandmother had never sent us anything. A few days later the box of apples arrived just as I had seen in my dream.

When I was eight years old, we attended our Roman Catholic parish church in Tuřany. At that time there was strict order in the church; the behaviour of children was sternly controlled. A crying baby was not tolerated. Men sat on the right side with boys in the front pews, and women on the left side with the girls in front. A man supervised the boys and a woman supervised the girls. Boys were disciplined by pulling their hair or their ears.

There was a boy about my age at the church who had polio. One of his legs was shorter than the other, and it was supported with a high heel boot and leather straps. I didn't like him because of his contorted mouth which I perceived as a sneer. One Sunday out of the blue when I was kneeling behind this boy, a clear voice spoke to me: "You are going to wear such a boot and straps."

My prompt answer was, "No! Never!"

The voice insisted, "Oh yes, you will!"

I was adamant. "No! Never!"

Two years later, I was fitted with a boot with ladder straps to support my left leg.

After the Munich international betrayal of Czechoslovakia in 1938, the Nazis occupied the defendable borders of the country, and in March, 1939, Czechoslovakia ceased to exist. The fear of the Gestapo, the concentration camps and the executions of Czech patriots became common. Every school classroom had a picture of Hitler on the front wall. The father of one of my classmates was executed. Many Czechoslovak military officers suffered the same fate.

The war was on. The winter of 1940 was harsh. My two siblings Joe and Margaret were hospitalized with scarlet fever. After a serious accident, my father required surgery on his left arm and was kept in hospital. My mother and I were left at home alone with four month old Tony and no source of income. There was no insurance; hunger, cold and depression filled our small apartment.

I was forbidden by my mother to go out. It was difficult for me to stay in this depressing atmosphere. Behind my mother's back, I picked up my skates and sneaked out to join a group of boys skating on the frozen road.

As we were chasing each other, a farmer approached us for help. He told us that his horse-drawn sleigh, filled with turnips, had overturned in a snow bank. All of us were eager to help, so we rushed to the accident scene. His wife held the reigns of the horses while the rest of us tried to push the overturned sleigh out of the snowbank. I was on the side of the sleigh beside the farmer. The restless horses suddenly jumped and pulled the half-lifted sleigh forwards about three feet. On my skates I slid under the sleigh. The side of the sleigh forced me deep into the snow, crushing my left femur under the hip. I didn't scream when they pulled me out from under the sleigh, but I wondered what happened to my leg. My crushed femur was pushed into my hip; the leg was shorter and my foot was turned 180 degrees backwards.

An ambulance arrived within half an hour and took me to the Children's Hospital in Brno. The anesthetist assured me that I would feel no pain because they would put me to sleep while they operated on my leg. Everything would be easy. I was impressed and believed him. When they placed a chloroform-sprayed cloth over my face, I started to choke. I became very angry because they had lied to me. Somehow by twisting my whole body, I freed my right arm, grabbed the cloth from my face, and threw it into the corner.

What followed was not pleasant. Someone slapped my face while the nurses restrained me. I woke up in my hospital bed vomiting and terrified of the anesthetic. I was in a cast from my waist to my toes, and my head ached. The narcotic was much worse than the pain in my leg.

After three weeks the cast was removed, but the leg had not healed. The medical staff, speaking German by my bed, decided on another operation after my parents signed a consent form. They had to cut my leg to get to the crushed bone. I didn't understand a word, but a boy next to me who spoke Czech and German told me what they said after they left. I was more afraid of the chloroform than of the surgery.

The next operation lasted four hours. When I awoke in my bed, I found myself in a cast again from my toes to my waist, unable to sit up, vomiting, and with a bad headache. Finally, after twelve weeks, I was liberated from the cast and could sit up. My left leg was skin and hair and stiff like a log. It was a bit shorter than the right leg.

I spent my eleventh birthday lying in the hospital in a bandage. After my release, it was decided, without my consent, that I would wear a boot with a high heel and straps around my damaged leg, just like the boy in the Tuřany church. My reaction was, "No! Never!" I would rather hobble around on one leg.

Using a string, I tied my mother's heavy iron to the damaged leg and pulled it behind me. It hurt, but I didn't give up. The leg had to be made longer and flexible. I wanted to be like the other boys again. My father was understanding and supportive of my efforts and my mother had no objections.

In school I was expected to repeat grade five since I had missed half the year. I protested. My father went to see the teachers, and they agreed to give me a chance in grade six. My marks were good and I wasn't behind in anything except German which I did not want to learn.

A year after the accident, the court resumed hearings against the poor farmer. I was a witness. My doctor stated that he expected me to be in a wheelchair by the age of thirty. He said that my recovery during the past year was a miracle. For my pain and suffering, the court awarded me a substantial amount of money that was deposited in my account, accessible when I turned twenty-one. I never saw a penny of the money because of the tumultuous situation with the war and then the communist takeover. Three years after the accident, I was skating again. I even played hockey.

4. Bookbinder

I WAS FOURTEEN WHEN I COMPLETED GRADE EIGHT. My last day in school was a happy one. On my way home, I threw my book bag high in the air and shouted, "Nobody will see me in school ever again."

In the summer of 1943, Hitler's army was in trouble on the Russian front, to the delight of many Czech patriots. Everyone who was fourteen had to work. The Arbeitsamt (Manpower Office) in Brno gave me three options for apprenticeship. My friend Alois and I chose to become bookbinders. I had to get up early every morning to catch the train to Brno at 6:15 a.m. and come home for supper at 6:00 p.m. As an apprentice, I had to attend an industrial school once a week for three years. I was back in school again.

My employer was Mr. Kotzian, whose family became German sometime during World War I, according to hearsay at his small factory of about twenty employees. He was a sociable and pleasant fellow about fifty years old, fluent in Czech and German. The layout of his factory was L-shaped, with two halls flowing into each other. The foreman was Mr. Bogdalek.

I smile when I remember my first day at work. I reported to Mr. Bogdalek and asked him what I was supposed to do. He gave me a cloth and instructed me to dust certain areas every morning. After I finished dusting, I came back to him and asked what was next. He showed me a set of wrenches and screwdrivers that he wanted cleaned, sorted and arranged in order. After I had finished that, I asked him for more work. He showed me several piles of paper glued together which had to be separated with a knife into piles that would be stapled individually. When I finished, I went back to him and he led me to the back of the second hall and glared at me.

"Sit down," he said. "I don't want to see you again."

I obediently sat down. After half an hour had passed, I found him and said, "I was sitting down as you instructed. Now what am I supposed to do next?" He shook his head and laughed.

I was used to physical work. As a small boy, I helped my mother with the household chores like hauling water, chopping wood, bringing coal up from the cellar, and looking after little Joe and Margaret. By the age of twelve I was helping my father in his painting business while other boys were playing. I felt sorry for myself, but I admired my father's skills, such as climbing high ladders, or depicting beautiful landscapes and village-life scenes with just his imagination and a paintbrush in hand. He was always happy while painting. He taught me how to make any shade of colour using white, yellow, blue, red and black.

At the bookbindery I learned all the skills used at Mr. Kotzian's establishment, ruling included. Ruling, which involved creating lines and columns for accounting practices, was a specialty beyond the competence of Mr. Bogdalek and Mr. Kotzian. Nobody in the factory could do this work except a specially trained seventeen-year-old named Franta Špaček. In spite of his innate intelligence, Franta had an aggressive, criminal mind. He was proud of his father who spent twenty years in jail. Nevertheless, Franta and I became friends. He didn't mind teaching me his ruling craft during lunch breaks.

At the beginning of 1945, Franta committed a crime for which he was about to be arrested by Gestapo. To avoid arrest, he intentionally injured himself and blamed it on the ruling machine. Only one other apprentice and I knew the truth. He was taken to the hospital, and then a convalescence period followed. He did not return to work, so Mr. Kotzian was forced to refer some of his customers to another firm. I went to see him and told him that I could take over Franta's job.

"Keep away from the ruling machine," he replied. "You must not touch it." Two days later, Mr. Kotzian came to me. "I'll give you an easy assignment so you can show me what you can do," he said. That assignment was so easy that I finished it in less than an hour. Mr. Kotzian was impressed.

He arranged for a skilled ruling expert to teach me about ruling. The gentleman asked me to show him what

I could do. In half-a-day I completed the most difficult tasks to his satisfaction. He reported to Mr. Kotzian that he had nothing more to teach me and that I could do everything. His certification meant a promotion, respect and some power. At any time I could call on four trained girls to assist me. I liked my new position.

Occasionally after work I would walk to the Brno railroad station with a girl, which surprised many of my teenage friends. Most of the boys were more handsome and attractive than I, but they were not so lucky.

My friends were apprentices of different crafts: cabinetmakers, locksmiths, watchmakers, and optometrists. In the evenings we formed a friendly group at the railroad station. The distance from Brno to Chrlice was about twenty minutes with two stops in between. We had two guitarists among us and we sang during our ride home. We became a close group who cared about each other.

Brno is an industrial city with an interesting history. The first serious attack on the city by American bombers was on November 20, 1944. They used carpet bombing and dropped bombs that exploded on the spot, as well as bombs that were timed to explode hours or even days later. They wreaked havoc on the city. Some streets disappeared, while others were reduced to rubble. Houses were in flames because of broken gas pipes, and sewage was pouring into the craters created by the bombs. Electricity was out and we were short of water. Cold and freezing rain followed. I found the situation exciting and got involved as an official volunteer with special markings on my sleeve. I was an authority. My task was to stop people from approaching the unexploded bombs. Smaller air attacks followed as the war went on.

In the spring of 1945, the Russian front was coming closer. Our last day at work in Brno was April 16. The end of the war was approaching, a tragic end for many German people, including Mr. Kotzian and his family. He lost two sons who were soldiers, and his brother was shot by a Russian soldier when the soldier saw his SA uniform. Mr. Kotzian's home was destroyed by a direct bomb strike. His factory was confiscated, and he and his family were exiled to Germany with their few possessions. It was cruel. Germany was in ruin and people worked just for food in order to survive.

I was hungry all the time. In a strange way, I enjoyed witnessing the war theatre. I got involved whenever I could. When most people were hiding in their cellars, I was out day and night. In all that horror there was also beauty: the flaming tails of the flying rockets, the thunder of cannons, the rosaries of shining bullets at night, the bombs in the blue sky falling on the Brno airport in the morning sun, planes shot down and pilots parachuting.

On one occasion six Messerschmitt (German Luftwaffe fighters) met with six Russian fighter planes right over my head. A spectacular, short dogfight followed. It was a show, yet it was real. Their machine guns were drumming and the planes were performing acrobatics for a minute or so, and then it was over. Both sides returned to the formations in which they had arrived and headed home, the Russians to the south, the Germans to the north. One of the Messerschmitts started to smoke and suddenly dropped like a stone. The pilot parachuted, his plane landing less than 150 metres from where I stood.

Another time, a Russian Ilushin, a light two-man crew bomber, was flying low, firing its two centimetre cannon and its two machineguns, one on each of its wings. Only after it was over did I realize what had happened. A bullet hit the wall four metres to my left, and the cannon shrapnel embedded in a brick wall two metres to my right.

When these images emerge in my mind after almost seventy years, I still feel the excitement. I did not experience paralyzing fear at that time. I wonder about my courage, my foolishness, and my good luck. The fact that I was only sixteen might explain it.

5. After the War

OUR GROUP OF TEENAGE APPRENTICES WAS JOINED by a few students after the war. Under the capable leadership of Leoš Davídek[1], our group changed into a more structured and disciplined Boy Scout troop. Besides camping and other Scouting activities, we built our own clubhouse, which was later confiscated by the communists.

We needed money. As the treasurer of the group, I squeezed small change from the pockets of my friends whenever I met them. I was amazed by how much money we accumulated in this way. However, it was not enough for our expenses, so we started putting on theatre performances. Artistically and financially we were successful, and I discovered that I had an acting talent. I was put into a few leading roles. I loved being on the stage, but my acting career was short-lived.

After the Communist party took over the government in February, 1948, their local branch became interested in our group. A professional older actress, a communist, started to attend our rehearsals to teach us about acting, and at the same time to influence us for the Marxist-Leninist cause.

We realized that we were in trouble. We hadn't done anything wrong, but it was obvious that the Communist party didn't like the Scouting ideals of self-reliance and independence. They wanted to get us into their own national youth organization, called Svaz Československé Mládeže (Union of the Czechoslovak Youth and their Pioneer). In many respects, this organization was similar to Scouts and to the Nazis' Hitler Jugend (Hitler Youth).

In the fall of 1946 at the age of seventeen, I passed my final industrial examination in front of three master bookbinders. I was now a professional bookbinder. On top of that, I was a ruling expert with a salary sufficient for raising a family. As I supervised the ruling work done by young women, two questions kept emerging in my mind: *Is this all there is to my life? What's next ... marriage?*

Although I liked small children and had experience looking after my younger brothers and sisters, I thought being married would mean being stuck in my present work for the rest of my life. No, marriage was not for me yet! There must be more to life, but what? I did not know.

My father was a frustrated and angry man, angry at the world and angry with me. He saw me as a trouble-maker who was, according to his religious standards, becoming corrupt and disrespectful. He felt that I needed to be a submissive "holy boy." That was not how I felt. I thought I was fine and doing better financially than he was. I gave all my income to my mother who was happy and appreciative. For more than year, she was in a better financial position than ever before.

My father wanted me out of the house, but I refused to move. He started bugging me about attending a religious retreat, but I was not interested. Finally, in September, 1947, I agreed to attend a retreat to get him off my back.

6. Conversion

I THOUGHT I'D BE ABLE TO SURVIVE THE THREE retreat days. Actually, I didn't know what a retreat even was, except that it was something "churchy."

The retreat was run by a fifty-year-old Jesuit, Father Nesrovnal,[2] in an old abandoned seminary building in Brno. The retreat started on Friday evening and ended on Monday afternoon. There were about twenty young men in attendance, all around my age. I was curious, and I liked the masculinity of the retreat-master—nothing feminine, except for wearing a cassock. His talks were clear, logical, emotional and to the point. They were based on down-to-earth life experiences, particularly experiences with the Nazis, university students' families, and students executed in the concentration camps.

In his opening remarks, Father Nesrovnal challenged the group: "There are three categories of people who come for Ignatian retreats. The first category is people who have planned and want to be here, and they are welcomed. The second category is those who've come to the retreat as one of their devotions. If there are any such people here, you should pack and go home. The third category have come by some coincidence, almost against your will. You will make the best retreatants and are heartily welcomed."

I knew at once which category I fell into.

The first thing the Jesuit taught us was how to pray. He explained that we should determine a time when we would pray, keep that time, and not hurry. We should begin with the Our Father prayer. Say "Our Father" and think about it. Think about what the word "Our" means. Don't just think, but also feel it, hear it, taste the word. Stay with it until the meaning and the feelings of the word are exhausted. Then go to the word "Father" and do the same thing. As long as your thoughts and emotions about these two words have meaning for you and feed you, give you joy, peace and satisfaction, stay with them. Do not go any further. Only after the feeling and meaning stop, go to the next words, "who art in heaven." Repeat the same method while pondering these words. Do not rush! If it takes one hour to go through the first sentence of the Our Father, it's better than if you say ten Our Fathers. Stick to the allotted time, even if you feel uncomfortable. When the time is over, it is over. End your prayer, even if you want to pray more.

I had never heard anyone talk about prayer that way, although by the age of ten, under the influence of my father, I had memorized 170 questions and answers of the catechism. I wondered if what the retreat master said was true. I decided to put it to the test.

Sometime around midnight, after everybody had gone to bed, I tiptoed from the common sleeping hall into the dark, empty chapel with the Blessed Sacrament in the tabernacle and the small red light beside it. I sat down in silent darkness and began.

"So, God, are you here or not? I need to know. I will do as the retreat master told us, and then I'll see if this kind of prayer works. I want to know whether or not he was telling the truth. It's up to You, God, to let me know if You are here or not." And so I began. "Our Father."

What followed was a cornerstone spiritual experience that is alive in me today. That retreat took place in September, 1947—sixty-five years ago. Yes, God exists, and He is a Father... Father of us all. He is Somebody, not something; He is living and is with us. He is here; He cares about us. We are His children—His children invited to be like Him. It's possible to speak to Him and He answers in various ways. He answers with deep, gentle feelings. Seldom He answers with words, but sometimes He does. He answers, but not always. He answered me!

I don't know how much time passed, but I remember that I didn't get beyond the two first words of the Our Father. A life-giving certainty arose in my heart. New horizons opened. From that moment on, I became fully involved in the rest of the retreat. I devoured every word the retreat master spoke.

The question of what I would do with my life came to my mind again. The retreat master talked about the shortage of men going into the priesthood. I listened with intere, even though I thought the subject had nothing to do with me. Eventually, though, another question emerged in my mind: *Why not me? Why shouldn't I serve this wonderful God in a special way?* To that question I answered, *That's not for me.*

I conjured up every argument I could against becoming a priest. I lacked an academic education, and I didn't want to go to school again. I did not like school. My mother depended on my income, and I didn't want to walk around in skirts like the priests. I couldn't possibly learn Latin. And so it went ... arguing in my mind.

But then words welled up inside of me:

"Look, you are free and you are being asked, not told, what to do. I am your God, and what is impossible for you is possible for me, if you accept my offer. Make up your mind which way you want to go, and then you and I will make a deal."

This inner conversation went through my mind the whole day, until I finally thought to myself: *I'd be stupid not to serve in a special way such a great God of joy, peace, and power.* Even though I still felt it was impossible for me to become a priest, I went for the deal.

"Okay," I said to God, "for my part, I'll do my best to become a priest. And you, God, must show me what you can do. You'll see that this project will fail."

The answer to my challenging words was a simple "okay."

The matter was settled, and I was at peace. It was now up to me to do my part to become a priest and to serve as a good and authentic one. It meant I had to start studying. It was up to me to give up my employment and go back to school without money or resources, depending entirely on good people with strong faith.

I entered into the darkness of my future. Here I am, Lord!

II. STRUGGLES BEGIN

7. Communist Takeover and Father Davidek

I GOT MYSELF INTO TROUBLE WITH MY SPIRIT OF self-confidence. After my spiritual conversion, I started to take religious observances seriously and let my co-workers know about it. I became a zealot.

Towards the end of February, 1948, the Communist party took over Czechoslovakia. The Soviet ambassador in Prague at that time was Mr. Zorin, a ruthless Russian diplomat, manipulator, and the right hand of Stalin. The elected president of Czechoslovakia was Dr. Eduard Beneš. He was hesitant to sign and approve the new communist Prime Minister, Klement Gottwald. To show its power and to scare the president, the Communist party organized a strike in most factories across the country.

A friendly Communist party member came to our bookbindery to supervise our strike. I was opposed to the Marxist-Leninist scientific atheism, so when the sirens of larger factories in Brno sounded a signal for the beginning of the strike, I was the only one in our plant who refused to co-operate. After all, I was a worker and nobody had asked me if I wanted to strike. In fact, nobody asked any of us if we wanted to strike. The strike was an imposition. I started my ruling machine and ordered my assisting women to work with me. They were happy to return to their work.

Mr. Bogdálek, the foreman with whom I had a good relationship, immediately stopped my machine. As soon as he left, I started the machine again and few other employees also started to work. Mr. Bogdálek returned very upset and reprimanded me.

"Don't you see that we are being watched?" he demanded. "You're just a young boy, but I have a family. Stop it!"

Annoyed, but out of respect for him as the foreman and a family man, I stopped my machine.

The next day I was ordered to the ROH (Revolutionary Trade Union) headquarters, a communist workers union of which I was not a member. To maintain a good relationship with my fellow workers, I attended the meeting. An old idealistic communist had a fatherly talk with me, an irrational and stubborn young man. He told me how he and his comrades used to be persecuted and humiliated for the cause of social justice. He explained that we were finally going to have true justice and plenty of everything. His party was in charge, and they would provide for all people equally and justly. He believed it; I did not, but his fatherly tone and good heart touched me. I sympathized with him, but I did not budge. At the end of our meeting, he warned me that the Communist party would have to re-educate me if I continued to make trouble. "On Sundays, you have to work like everybody else," he said. I ignored his warning, and on Sunday I stayed at home. That happened for two subsequent Sundays.

Mr. Bogdálek liked me and meant well; however, he was the foreman and responsible for making all employees work on Sundays. Working on Sundays was a communist tool to break the quiet and restful observance of the third commandment of the Jewish decalog, accepted by the Christians as their own.

Mr. Bogdálek started calling me a religious fanatic. I told him that I was reasonable and not a fanatic, and that I was prepared to work on Sundays provided there was a real need for it, but I did not see any such need.

"Such a need really exists," he insisted.

I didn't believe him, but I had no proof to the contrary. He told me that certain orders must be delivered to the customers on Monday, so everybody must work on the coming Sunday. Well, that gave me no other choice but to come to work on Sunday. I assured Mr. Bogdálek that he could count on me for the coming Sunday. At the same time, I told him that if he were playing games with me, he wouldn't see me on a Sunday again. Nothing was delivered on Monday.

That was it! I was left with only two choices: co-operate and work on Sundays or be arrested as an enemy of the people and sent to a Marxist-Leninist re-education labour camp. Now what? What was I going to do? I needed to resolve this dilemma and make a decision.

Easter week began on Palm Sunday. Everything slowed down, including the Communist party machinery and their police. The religious and cultural tradition of Easter festivities affected even the general membership of the Communist party. A cultural tradition was a cultural tradition, even if it was religious. Many old communists were well meaning communists with naive beliefs in a social justice achievable by their "scientific" atheistic ideology and practice.

On the Monday after Palm Sunday, I learned that a young priest, Father Felix Davídek, was visiting with his parents in Chrlice. I went to see him to discuss my situation. We sat on a bench in his family's large garden and talked about the political situation in Czechoslovakia. While stuttering, Father Felix invited me to come to Horní Štěpánov, where he was an assistant to the old parish priest, Father Buček, a former patriotic soldier in Russia and a legionary in World War I. Felix sensed a danger too, and said that he needed to leave Czechoslovakia for the West. He invited me to join him, and we agreed that I would come to Horní Štěpánov on Easter Saturday. He promised that on Easter Monday, after he celebrated Holy Mass, both of us would cross the border illegally into Austria. It shouldn't be difficult, he assured me, because he had good friends on the Austrian border who would help us.

I didn't know anything about Horni Štěpánov except that it was a village somewhere in the hills north of Chrlice. Felix explained how to get there. After I arrived at Šebetov by train, I was to walk through the forest for about an hour to Pohora, a small village known as a partisan base during World War II. From there it wasn't far to Štěpánov.

On Easter Saturday, with tears in my eyes and under false pretenses, I said goodbye to my parents and my younger siblings. I did not tell my parents where I was going, except that I would be with Father Felix for Easter Sunday. That was acceptable to them. They didn't know that I was about to leave Czechoslovakia. I thought that my goodbye would only be for several years until communism collapsed or was defeated in a war. If a war should take place, I would return home as a victorious soldier or a priest. That was the way I imagined it.

Following Felix´s instructions, I took the train to Šebetov and walked to Horni Štěpánov. Passing through the forest, I noticed the rusting cannons and a Panzer tank left behind by the retreating German army. It was late in the afternoon and the sky was cloudy.

Horní Štěpánov was situated in a valley with a neglected windmill in the background. When I saw the windmill, I realized I was closer to the village than I expected. A jubilant procession was exiting from the church singing, "Long live the Victor over death who was raised alive from his grave," a joyful Czech church hymn which I knew.

As an outsider, I didn't want to be noticed by the people in the procession. I sat down in the snow in a ditch and waited until the landscape became dark and the village quiet. Then I went in. I entered the old rectory and asked for Father Felix. He immediately came and welcomed me with a smile. Later that evening, he led me to the Přikrylovi family. There was a festive atmosphere in their house. After a delicious supper served by Mrs. Přikrylova, Felix returned and led me to the house of Mrs. Pluháček, where I could stay until Monday.

Mrs. Pluháček, a fifty-five-year-old widow, had a son named Josef, four years older than I, who wanted to become a priest. He admired Felix and would do anything for him. Felix confided in Josef about practical matters and used his services extensively. The whole village of Horní Štěpánov lived in a strong, traditional Roman Church religious culture with the exception of a few local communists. Some of them used to attend church regularly.

On Easter Monday, Felix explained that we would have to delay our departure for Austria for a week because he had some important business on his hands. Meanwhile, I could stay with Mrs. Pluháček and get my meals with the Přikrylovi family.

What was supposed to be a brief layover in Horní Štěpánov turned into eighteen months. During this time, under Felix's supervision, I had been studying to complete my high school requirements. Since I was penniless, the Přikrylovi family and Mrs. Pluháček took care of me. Many times I felt uncomfortable taking advantage of these good people, but I rationalized my feelings by telling God and myself that it was not my doing that I was in such a situation. I was on a spiritual path of obedience and self-giving.

8. Horní Štěpánov

LATE ONE AFTERNOON AFTER ABOUT A YEAR AT Horní Štěpánov, I came home to Mrs. Pluháček's house to find a uniformed police officer waiting with a warrant for my arrest. My stomach convulsed. *That's it!* I panicked. *The communists found me and they've got me.* With trembling hands I gave the officer my identification document, but the date of birth on the warrant didn't correspond to my personal document's birth date. The officer explained that there must be another Jiří Hořák,[3] so he would not arrest me. He left and I was greatly relieved. I told Felix about the incident, but it didn't impress him; he just smiled. My studies with Felix could continue.

Felix used to say: "I am working with what God sends me. I cannot work with something that is desirable but does not exist." He had in mind better students. He gradually enlarged our initial group of four with country boys who became his followers. He was a demanding teacher. For example, he wanted me to analyze poems loaded with symbols and explain the poet's vision of more subtle levels of reality. Most students couldn't do it. From several of his students, including me, he required readings such as Fjodor M. Dostoyevsky's *Brothers Karamasov* and

The Idiot, or Miguel de Cervantes Saredra's *Don Quixote de la Mancha.* Gilbert K. Chesterton's *The Ball and the Cross* and Dostoyevsky's *The Idiot* left a lasting impression on me.

Felix also directed a group of four young girls, of which Vlasta was the most prominent. Later in her life, Dr. Vlasta Černá served as a clinical psychologist. Felix loved this young beauty. I still communicate with Vlasta to this day. She became a widow after her husband, a psychiatrist, died.

Not long before the warrant incident, Vilém, my old friend from Boy Scouts in Chrlice, joined me in Horní Štěpánov without his parents being aware of it. At my prompting, he made a retreat with the same Jesuit as I did. He decided to follow me towards the priesthood. Before he came to Horní Štěpánov, he was an apprentice in optometry and lived in a residence away from his family. His parents supported him financially by regularly sending money to the residence. Vilém arranged for the residence to continue forwarding the money to him in Horní Štěpánov.

On a beautiful summer morning in 1949, Vilém and I were walking back from daily mass. He told me about a vivid, disturbing dream. His parents had discovered that he was not living at the student residence and studying optometry, but instead was with Felix and me in Horní Štěpánov. The next morning he told me that his dream continued, but had a happy ending. The third day all hell broke loose. Indeed, what he dreamed came true. His mother arrived and confronted Felix at the rectory in Vilém's presence, shouting and screaming at Felix. She blamed him for encouraging her son's deception and disrespect towards his parents. What a scandalous priest Felix was! Shame on him!

After the incident, Mrs. Juza immediately returned home to Chrlice, leaving Vilém in Horní Štěpánov. Vilém refused to go with her. In spite of it all, Vilém was not rejected by his parents; the door of his home in Chrlice remained opened for him. Mrs. Juza was generous with me, inviting me to visit any time. I did not know why. In her eyes, both of us were misguided, misled, and stubborn teenagers under the influence of a bad priest. We deserved her understanding and acceptance. The storm cleared and it was easy to breathe again. For a short time we were left to study in peace.

I had no money. I was poor, but I had a spirit of confidence and enthusiasm. Tonda Grenar and Láďa Vařeka were in our initial group of students. Láďa was a highly intelligent fellow. His father was a tailor and an old fashioned, idealistic communist—a good man and a friend. He told me about his disappointment with the Roman Catholic Church when a Capuchin priest at a mission in Horní Štěpánov humiliated and rejected him publicly by shouting at him in the wooden confessional box surrounded by a group of penitent people. He called him a pig. Everybody in the church heard it. The man had five children and could no longer adequately support his family, so he and his wife had started to practice birth control, which was considered a mortal sin.

At that time, there was a branch of a Catholic cultural and gymnastic organization called Orel (Eagle) in Horní Štěpánov. Shortly after the war, the Horní Štěpánov chapter of Orel built a large, well designed gym that served various purposes such as gymnastics, wedding celebrations, theatre performances and dances. The local communists, with the help of police, confiscated the hall for themselves. They removed the cross and replaced it with pictures of Stalin and Gottwald. One night somebody broke into the hall, removed the pictures, threw them on the floor and defecated on them. It made me laugh and angry at the same time because I knew that the group around Felix would be the first target of the police investigation. And so it was.

Police cars arrived. I was arrested and interrogated while a German shepherd barked at me. I had tears in my eyes. I didn't have much to say, except that I disagreed with this primitive but powerful anti-government gesture.

At that time not all police officers were communists. Some of them co-operated with the government in order to protect their jobs. I felt that the incident was the end of me. I never would be able to leave the country and study for the priesthood. I had done my best, but I could do no more. Now I might be sent to a re-education labour camp. In my mind, it was Felix´s fault because he had not kept his promise to leave the country for Austria at Easter in 1948. The police ordered some of Felix's students who were not from Horní Štěpánov to leave town at once. However, for reasons unknown to me, the police released me and let Vilém stay at Horní Štěpánov.

Not long after that episode, Vilém´s father confronted him. He told Vilém that he was stupid and immature. If Vilém wanted to be a priest, then he would accept it, in spite of the fact that Vilém was not cut out for the celibate priesthood in his father's opinion. If Vilém was aiming for the seminary, then he should act with integrity and not deceive his parents. His father did some research and went to meet with Bishop Trochta.[6]

Bishop Trochta accepted Vilém into his seminary in Litoměřice, administered by its rector, a former Capuchin priest named Rabas. I felt abandoned by Vilém and left alone in Horní Štěpánov. I didn't feel ready for the seminary. In my mind, I knew that it was necessary to enter into the five-year seminarian academic program, but I believed it would happen later on, not now.

Two weeks after Vilém's departure, I received a threatening letter from the Manpower Office in Olomouc, a former metropolitan city of Moravia. Horní Štěpánov was under its jurisdiction. The letter ordered me to report for work at the coal mines in the city of Ostrava. If I didn't show up on the date specified in the letter, I would be taken there by police.

With the letter in hand I went to see Felix, reminding him of his promise to leave our communist controlled country. He replied that my situation was not his concern; I had to deal with it myself. I felt betrayed and hurt, but there was no time to dwell on my feelings. I had to act without delay.

I returned from the rectory to Mrs. Pluháček´s home, said a prayer to the Holy Spirit as my mother taught me, and read the letter several times. Finally, a solution emerged in my mind. I wrote a letter to the Manpower Office, apologizing for not being able to report to the coal mines on time. I said that I was prepared to co-operate, but their order came too late, namely after the date when I was supposed to be in Ostrava. I pointed out that they had made an administrative mistake because I belonged to the Brno Manpower Office, not the Olomouc one. Obviously, the trap for me was prepared by the ignorant communist chapter in Horní Štepánov.

I mailed the letter, packed my belongings in a large suitcase, asked Felix for enough money for a railroad ticket, and dragged the suitcase through the forest to the Šebetov's railroad station. At midnight I rang the bell at the main entrance of the seminary in Litoměřice. I did so because I felt I had to disappear from Horní Štěpánov at once and not return to my parents' home in Nedašov where the police could easily find me.

Father Veselka, the vice-rector of the seminary, came to the door. I told him I wanted to be a priest, and that I already had a close friend in the seminary, Vilém, who could testify to my identity and sincerity. Father Veselka found it strange that someone without a reference would come to the seminary at midnight wanting to become a priest. He let me in and said he would make his decision in the morning. Vilém was glad to see me. I was admitted without money, but with caution.

Bishop Trochta at that time had enough influence to protect his seminarians from the police. He was respected by some of the top Czech communist leaders, who knew him well from the Nazi concentration camps as a courageous and caring man. If police were after one of Trochta's people, he could call his Czech communist friends, and the police would back off. This situation was only temporary. The powerful Czech communist leaders were not as powerful as they pretended. The real leadership and direction came from the Soviet ambassador Zorin, probably a member of the International Communist Party in Moscow. The Czech and Slovak "leaders" were only the idealistic and obedient, but reckless puppets who executed Moscow's orders.

For the time being, however, I was safe under the protective wing of Bishop Trochta. I could continue my studies that I started under Felix in Horní Štěpánov. God was doing His/Her part in our 1947 contract and I was doing mine.

9. Seminary in Litoměřice

THERE I WAS, IN THE LITOMĚŘICE SEMINARY WITH
seventy-five future priests. I had no money to support
myself. After Father Nesrovnal, the Jesuit retreat master
from Brno, learned about my whereabouts, he made
arrangements with the Czechoslovak Catholic Women
and Maidens' League to pay for my seminary expenses.

A large group of seminarians had not completed high
school, so the seminary provided several high school
teachers, all of them priests, to prepare us for the final
Gymnasium (High School) maturity exam. Thanks to
Felix, Vilém and I had been registered for all examina-
tions at the Gymnasium na Poříčí in Brno while we lived
in Horní Štěpánov. In addition to the high school courses,
we attended several courses in philosophy and theology.

In the spring of 1950, some of Felix's other students
saw that there was a door open for them at the Litoměřice
seminary. Two of them, Stanislav Florian and Josef
Krajíček, were advanced enough in their Gymnasium
studies that they could join us at the seminary. Felix,
accompanied by Vlasta, came to visit our Horní Štěpánov
group of four at the seminary. He criticized the seminary's academic program, and by coming with an attractive young woman to the large assembly of celibate

clergy, he created a bad impression. After they left, Felix was reproved by two scandalized Salesian priests in front of all the seminarians gathered in the chapel. I felt quite uncomfortable, but I doubted the criticism would concern Felix.

The communist government was gradually tightening its grip on the Roman Catholic Church and on other Christian denominations. One night, the police unexpectedly confiscated clergy files at bishops' residences across the country. Based on these files, they assessed individual priests as zealous, influential, passive, or sick and old. The zealous and influential ones had to be removed from their pastoral ministry and incarcerated immediately. It was important for the communists to create an impression of religious freedom in a country governed by them. Except for individuals interested in international religious and political matters, their propaganda succeeded among the general world population.

Bishop Trochta[4] was placed under house arrest in the spring of 1950. Plain clothes police officers controlled his activities and contacts and did not allow him to leave his residence. They stayed with him day and night. However, before his trial, his close collaborators, the seminary rector Rabas and his vicar general Vlk, were allowed to visit him. The limited freedom that the bishop enjoyed before his sentencing allowed him to do a few things. According to the Church's canon law at that time, baptized Roman Catholics belonged to the diocese in which they were born. They were the diocesan bishop's subjects. If they wanted to become a cleric in another diocese, they needed the approval of their bishop. They would become a cleric not by ordination, but by tonsura, a rite which involved the bishop symbolically cutting the candidate's hair.

Many of us seminarians in Litoměřice legally belonging to other dioceses. The house-arrested Bishop Trochta was secretly incardinating us by the rite of the tonsura into his Litoměřice diocese in his residential chapel. The plain clothes police officers present were told that what the bishop was doing was a customary and traditional devotion that required the presence of the seminarians. The officers witnessed the "devotion" and didn't see anything dangerous in it. Small groups of seminarians were coming and going for the "devotion." And so I was incardinated from the diocese of Brno into the diocese of Litoměřice. I doubt that there is a church document recording the event.

Under the influence of Felix's thinking, it was clear to me that the communists' systematic work against the Church would not relent but would become even more effective. I kept speaking about the sinister communist approach to some of the seminarians, but except for a few individuals, I didn't find much support. The majority did not see the situation as dangerous. Nobody seemed willing to risk his freedom or even his life, by leaving the country illegally in order to become a priest. I remember a monsignor who rejected my assessment as exaggerated. He had two PhDs, but was rather naïve.

"We Czechs are a cultural nation," he stated. "We are not like the Russians. The communist rule will be over soon; it cannot last. The Americans will come to liberate us. They already started a war against the communists in Korea."

To me, the coming ecclesiastical disaster was obvious and unavoidable. Towards the end of May, 1950, the house-arrested Bishop Trochta, through his seminary's rector Rabas, gathered all of us seminarians in the chapel to inform us that very probably all seminaries in the country would be closed by the Czechoslovak government. Two new seminaries would be opened in the autumn under the direction and supervision of the Communist party—one in Bohemia, and the other in Slovakia. Father Rabas advised us to co-operate with the government in non-substantial matters, so as not to give the communists any real pretext to close our seminary. And so we co-operated.

One morning the agricultural union of farm workers sent a truck to the seminary. Under the direction of Father Rabas, we boarded the truck in our clerical outfits so the public could see what was happening. We were driven to a large potato field to work. The public was indifferent toward us. Wearing our clerical outfits on a large agricultural truck, we did not make much of an impression on anybody. Most people seemed apathetic.

We were working together with women workers who cheerfully treated us as comrades. My back ached. At the end of the day, they prepared a good meal for us. They were good, simple people who believed in the ideal of communist social justice. After supper we boarded the truck again, and returned to the seminary.

Our co-operation didn't have an impact on the communists. The government probably assumed that Trochta and Rabas would refuse to expose their seminarians to the humiliation. It would provide public proof that the Catholic clergy were allies of the capitalistic West and enemies of working people.

Later on, Father Rabas gathered all of us again in the chapel and instructed us in the name of our bishop: "If indeed all the seminaries are closed, no one should enter a communist seminary. Theology based on the atheist Marxist-Leninist ideology is unthinkable, and should not be taught. If any seminarian enters the new seminary, Bishop Trochta and I will refuse to recognize him." Father Rabas continued: "Our bishop expects to be disabled by permanent incarceration. Possibly under mental and physical torture, he might change his mind and ask his seminarians to return to the new communist seminary. In that case, the bishop's request will be invalid, and all seminarians should ignore it. Only if the request is contrasigned by five priests should the request be considered as valid, and the seminarians should return in September. All of you will be notified during the summer vacation whether or not the seminary will be closed, and whether or not you should return in September." Obviously our bishop had access to a leak from the Communist party headquarters in Prague. Eventually he was sentenced to twenty-five years in prison.

The house-arrested Trochta gave his consent for the communists to give the seminarians in Litoměřice a one-week course in Marxist-Leninist doctrine. The course was about the communist government creating peace and happiness for all humanity by placing their symbolic red flag on the North Pole. The course took place in the seminary at the beginning of June, 1950, and was delivered in the form of a religious retreat. I learned quite a bit from the sessions.

There were two instructors for the course. One of them claimed to be from the Faculty of Philosophy at Karlova Universita in Prague. Both men were quite knowledgeable. Their communism was idealistic, abstract and academic. They dealt with subjects like social injustice, capitalism, power struggles, politics, and foreign intelligence. On several occasions, I felt that they hoped to enlist some of us into their foreign intelligence service if we could be convinced of their noble cause.

The instructors spoke with conviction and encouraged us to ask questions and debate with them. It did not work. No questions came from the seminarians. No debate. My main problem with them was their openly professed atheism and their almost religious faith that mere humanism and science would solve all existing problems. What follows are some of their views.

To establish themselves as the world government, the communists would have to provoke revolutions in non-communist countries. Revolutions would be an important tool against all non-communist governments. Marxist-Leninism, or communism, must not be professed where it would be counter-productive. The focus would be on local problems like nationalism, poverty, religion, or anything else that would create confusion, tension and a revolutionary atmosphere.

Intelligence agents would be hidden in low employment positions such as taxi drivers or porters to study the local situation and resources. They would befriend and support the local agitators and their cause by providing them with ideas and resources, but the agent would keep hidden in the background.

An intelligence officer would guide the local revolutionaries in creating unrest and confusion in the non-communist society using local people. Use of weapons must be avoided, but if the situation called for weapons, the Communist party would provide them. The local agitators would believe they were the leaders. Agents would assist them as needed, but would continue to stay in the background, being friendly and available for consultation and planning. The local people would provide the agents with information valuable to the leadership of the party.

The main focus would be on university campuses and women, not so much on men, since the majority of men are conservative and do not want change. However, the men must be made to believe they are important, that they are the true revolutionaries. Once the foundation for a revolution was laid, then men would be sent into the streets with sticks.

If the local revolution succeeded, all its leaders would be gradually removed within two years, and new leaders with administrative skills and loyal to the communist cause would take their place. The former local revolutionary leaders would become dangerous to the new establishment because they would eventually criticize and rebel again, this time against the communist system.

Years later, when I lived in foreign countries, I wondered about the various global political situations, particularly in places like Ireland or Quebec, where French nationalists and university students pushed for separation from Canada. It was no surprise for me years ago to read in a newspaper about a Czechoslovak ship delivering hydraulic pumps to the Irish. When the British searched the ship, they found weapons and ammunition in the wooden pump boxes. Actually, I thought, the communist infiltrating system could be used with some adjustments by any powerful organization seeking control over the world by gradually undermining local governments.

Today, after many years of experience, I cannot avoid thinking about my spiritual mother, the Roman Catholic

Church. Officially and structurally even today, it is led by a strong conservatism natural to men attempting to silence assertive women. A certain amount of conservatism and tradition is necessary, but not too much because our modern society is changing too quickly.

The academic communists seemed to know something about women and about their enthusiasm and practical hard work for a cause in which they believed. They recognized their feminine influence and power and their leadership qualities. They knew that common men have a subconscious fear of women and therefore try to keep them in subordinated positions. With modern higher education and communication available to everybody, the centuries old patriarchal conservative attitude is no longer viable. Educated women have proven many times that they are intellectually equal and sometimes superior to equally educated men. In this respect, our conservative church needs to learn something from the educated, theoretically oriented communist professors and artists.

As expected, communism finally discredited itself, collapsed, and for the most part is now history across Europe. Its attractive theory of social equality and justice systematically ignored sinful human nature; that is, it ignored human egoism, self-centredness, and selfishness rooted in fear and anxiety. These negative psychological dimensions of our human existence did not collapse. They continue to flourish in our modern society, but under different auspices. Pure rationalism with its analytical and logical approach to material reality is useful and necessary in science and technology, but without the human spiritual higher mind, it is incapable of dealing with human existence or with the higher self in each of us.

While in Nedašov with my parents that August, I received a typed, unsigned notification: "Seminary closed. Do not return!" I later learned that six seminarians returned rather than be enlisted for three years of service in military uniforms without weapons, but with picks and shovels for manual work. I refused to go to Mimoň, a military base, where the Czechoslovak army commanded all seminarians to gather for "obligatory military service."

10. Hunted by Police

I FEARED THE STATE SECURITY (STB), THE COMMU-
nist police. I considered them my personal enemies. On
two occasions they arrested me, and twice they let me
go. I didn't know why they let me go until I worked as
a probation and parole officer with the criminal justice
system in Canada. Some key criminals are left free for
a time because they are useful in leading police to other
individuals that are of interest.

Towards the end of June, 1950, Vilém and I completed
our final Gymnasium Maturity examination in Brno.
When Vilém and I left the school building on that beautiful sunny afternoon, our friend Stanislav Florian was
waiting for us. He showed us the handcuff marks on his
wrists and told us the following story.

Stan and Arnold, both students of Felix, accompanied Felix to the railroad station in Šebetov. When they
arrived at the station, the police appeared, arrested
all three of them, and drove them to the police station.
After the officers interrogated them individually, they got
into their cars and drove to Felix's apartment in Horní
Štěpánov, leaving the three prisoners in custody.

Felix needed to go to the bathroom, but the toilet was
located on the first floor. The entrance to the building was

locked, and the officer had no objection to letting Felix go. Obviously, he viewed Felix as a timid and trustworthy priest. When Felix did not return after a long time, the easygoing officer sent one of the boys to retrieve him. Stan knocked on the bathroom door, calling, "Reverend Father! Reverend Father!" He felt that Felix was up to something so he did not try to open the door. He reported to the officer that Felix was not answering. Felix, a small man, had squeezed through the washroom window, jumped down and escaped into the nearby woods.

When the officer saw the open window and Felix gone, he was angry and ordered the two boys to help him search the building before he called his superiors to report that the prisoner had escaped. The other officers returned from Horní Štěpánov at once, handcuffed the two boys, and started their interrogation again. The next morning, they sent both boys home.

Stan didn't go home, but came to see Vilém and me instead.

"What are we going to do now?" he asked. He explained that Felix was very lucky because when he jumped from the window, he landed on cement so there were no tracks indicating the direction he had gone. He was also fortunate because it started to rain, preventing the police dogs from tracking him. I suggested to Stan and Vilém to keep calm and wait and see what happened next.

It was clear to me that I was in trouble again. How could I escape from Czechoslovakia without having the necessary connections to some underground organization? Felix had contacts, but I didn't know where he was. I had to find him.

I assumed that Vlasta, his seventeen-year-old girlfriend from Horní Štěpánov, would know where he was. She did, but she wouldn't tell me anything. Indirectly she turned my attention to a family in Horní Štěpánov by visiting it frequently. That family knew of my close association with Felix and trusted me. I pretended that I knew that Felix was hiding in their house. They revealed that Felix had been there, but had moved the previous day to a neighbouring village disguised as a woman. Horní Štěpánov had become too dangerous for him. One member of that family was a religious sister belonging to a modern Congregation of Těšitelky (Consolers), with their Mother House in Rajhrad.

For a few days I stayed with my friend Mrs. Pluháček in Horní Štěpánov. From her and from one of her neighbours, I learned that the secret police were looking for Felix in the late afternoon around Horní Štěpánov. I underestimated the women's stories, laughing them off as exaggerations. I didn't think the government would waste police manpower on catching a young village priest. I was mistaken.

The morning after learning that Felix was in Pavlov, I went to meet him. He was living in a small room with a window facing trees. His hosts were simple country people with a strong faith and a great respect for priests.

Their daughter Žofka, a Gymnasium student, belonged to the group of four female students directed by Felix. They welcomed me, and Felix was glad to see me. Before Felix and I discussed how to evade police and leave Czechoslovakia for the West, he celebrated Holy Mass.

Felix knew about three underground organizations, one of which was in Konice, not too far from Horni Stepanov. Before his arrest, Felix had medically helped the wife of Mr. Mikmek of Konice. Mr. Mikmek was a member of one of the three underground organizations known to Felix. The organizations did not know about each other, but Felix knew about all three. They were helping anti-communist people escape from the communist paradise. Mr. Mikmek, in gratitude to Felix for helping his wife, offered to help Felix if he got himself into difficulty with the communists.

In his current situation, Felix needed all the help he could get. In our planning session in Pavlov, he asked me to go to Konice and meet Mr. Mikmek. He told me where to find him. To prove to Mr. Mikmek that I was an authentic messenger from Felix, he gave me his old university student document. I then returned to Mrs. Plauháček in Horní Štěpánov.

The next day I borrowed a bicycle from one of Felix's students, and late in the afternoon I hit the road to Konice, about ten kilometres away. On the road at the edge of Horní Štěpánov, sat two cars with a German shepherd sitting behind the wheel of one car. There was also a motorcycle and a group of about six men in plain-clothes outside the cars smoking and chatting.

I panicked for a few seconds. I was riding right into the arms of the waiting police. The women were right! Now it was too late. I didn't know what to do except pray to my guardian angel. That all flashed through my mind very quickly. My instinct was to slowly continue on my way. I passed the group and nobody moved. They let me go—I couldn't believe it. I felt relieved; however, my disbelief and relief were short-lived.

A motorcycle followed me, keeping about one hundred metres behind me. Obviously the men had allowed me to pass because they wanted to know where I was going. Now what? My first reaction was to throw Felix's identification document into the ditch, but the inner voice told me not to.

"No! He sees you. He has a motorcycle, a radio and a handgun; he can catch up with you at any time. He will see you throwing something into the ditch he will find it. That will be the end not only of you, but also of Felix. Keep calm and leisurely continue on your way."

"Yes, but what am I going to do?" I questioned the inner voice.

"Pray and keep going!"

I kept going, thinking about my next move.

Just outside of Konice, the road sloped down significantly, crossed an intersection at the bottom, then passed under railroad tracks and curved towards the centre of the town. In April, 1945, the German Army (Wehrmacht) was retreating with their trucks and tanks on secondary roads where they were less visible to Soviet planes. They badly damaged the road which was now full of potholes. Because of the potholes, all vehicles had to slow down to avoid an accident. When I arrived at that unfamiliar section of the road, I thought, *This is it. This is your chance! The man behind you has to slow down while you have to risk everything and speed up, potholes or no potholes.* I was lucky I didn't have an accident.

Towards the end of the sloping road, before the railroad underpass on my left, stood a large building where I was supposed to meet Mr. Mikmek. As I passed the building, I noticed there wasn't an entrance from the road. I quickly concluded that the entrance must be on the other side. At the intersection before the underpass, I turned left and immediately left again, and there was the entrance.

The entrance was set back several metres into the building and surrounded by a grassy area. The area was enclosed by a two metre green living fence. I disappeared behind the fence. It all happened in a flash. I breathed a sigh of relief when the motorcycle didn't appear. Obviously, he got confused at the intersection and lost my trail. I rang the bell at the entrance of the Agriculture Cooperative building where Mr. Mikmek was the manager. A cleaning lady opened the door; I told her that I wanted to see Mr. Mikmek.

"Mr. Mikmek already left for home," she replied. "He has another office at home where you can find him." She gave me directions to his house which wasn't far away.

11. Happy Ending

I THANKED THE CLEANING LADY FOR THE DIREC-tions, returned to the intersection, counted the houses, and rang the doorbell. Mrs. Mikmek invited me in and led me to their courtyard where her husband was working in his office. Obviously she was used to his customers coming to their house.

Mr. Mikmek and I had never met. He was a distinguished, middle-aged man who was full of energy. I introduced myself and told him why I had come and what I wanted. To prove the authenticity of my mission, I produced Felix´s university document. While I looked at him with expectation, he studied my face in silence.

Without a word, he lifted the telephone receiver and started to dial. I placed my hand on his hand. "Mr. Mikmek, what are you doing? "

"I am calling your friends who will take you home."

"Do you mean the police?" I asked.

"Of course," he replied. "You arrested Felix, got his documents and now you're trying to get me into trouble. The police will deal with you."

"Mr. Mikmek, if you call STB, then you will have innocent blood on your hands. If your thinking is correct and I am a police agent, then the police already know what you're up to and what you're involved in. As a police agent, I could arrest you without acting out this comedy." He put the telephone down and was silent. After a few minutes, he called his wife and asked her to bring me something to eat.

Before his wife came back with milk and a slice of rye bread, he told me that the police knew about their Sokol and legionaries (Czech and Slovak army in Russia during World War I fighting against the Austrian empire) underground organization. Their operation in Konice had to stop all activities because after they saved their parish priest, Father Pitrun,[8] from incarceration and helped him escape to Czechoslovakia, the STB detachment in Konice was reinforced by more agents.

Then he continued. "You cannot go back from where you came because of your story about coming here. The police are after you and will catch you for sure. You must stay overnight, but not in my house. I have a family. I cannot take any more risks. You will sleep at my father-in- law's house which is nearby. When it is dark, my wife will lead you to her parents' house. You will follow a short distance behind her and enter the house that she will signal by waving her arm. My in-laws are old people and live alone."

I followed Mr. Mikmek's instructions and entered the house that his wife pointed out. The old couple knew I was coming. The gentleman led me immediately to their bedroom which had a large window that opened to the street. He ordered me to sit down below that window and keep quiet. He explained that several police officers were on evening patrols, looking into people's windows. He turned on the lights so that every by-passer could see that nothing was happening in the house. His wife brought me a basin of water to wash up. At about 10:00 p.m., we went to sleep. I slept in their bed with the old man while his wife slept in another room. Before the old fellow got into bed, he put a handgun under his pillow. I liked him; I trusted him. The old soldier was still alive in him. I felt secure in his hands and slept like a baby.

The next morning at five o'clock he woke me and told me to disappear from Konice before the police officers awoke from their nightshift. I rode the borrowed bike back to Horní Štěpánov. The sun was rising, the birds were singing, the air was fresh, and my heart was jubilant over the successful adventure.

When I reported my adventures to Felix in Pavlov, he was not disturbed at all; he just stuttered and smiled. We sat down to develop a new plan of action.

12. Znojmo

THE ANTI-COMMUNIST UNDERGROUND ORGANIZA-
tion in Konice failed us. At his hiding place in Pavlov,
Felix disclosed to me two other underground organizations helping people to illegally cross the border. One
originated in Rajhrad and the other in Znojmo. He
decided that I should go to Znojmo and organize things
from there. He gave me the address and the money I
needed for the train.

In Horní Štěpánov I met three brothers named Spáčil,
mature, respectable men. One lived in Horní Štěpánov
and was a teacher, the other was a parish priest, and the
third was a military man, a commander of border guards.
He and his family lived in the city of Znojmo close to the
Austrian border. All three were dedicated patriots.

When I entered the border guard commander's house
in Znojmo, I had no difficulty identifying myself. No
explanation was needed. The commander knew about
me. He instructed me not to take any notes on what he
was going to tell me, but to rely on my memory.

According to Commander Spáčil, there were still a
few places where it was possible to cross the border
without major problems, provided that one knew the
terrain. The barbed wire, electric fences and watchtowers

were under construction and not finished. There were still some patriots among the border guards who would close their eyes when they saw someone escaping to avoid imprisonment.

The commander, with a map on the table, explained that the terrain was rather flat and had a web of deep ditches from the nineteenth century vineyards. The purpose of the ditches was to drain water from the fields. Dyje, a nearby river, was the border between Czechoslovakia and Austria. He apologized for not being able to give me the map or allow me to make my own drawings of it. At the end of our meeting he said that he was expecting to be replaced by a communist commander. I left his house the next day at five in the morning.

When I met Felix in his hiding place, he did not like what I told him. He felt that Spáčil´s way might be confusing and too risky. It could be used, but only in absolute desperation. He sent me to Rajhrad.

I would like to add that Mr. Spáčil´s willingness to help was not entirely wasted. In Chrlice I had a neighbour named Josef Kříž, whom I'd known well since childhood. In the summer of 1950, his class had graduated from Gymnasium. All those who had passed the final examination celebrated their graduation with an evening party. Perhaps under the influence of too much alcohol, some boys became too noisy and were making ridiculing remarks about the new communist regime. Somebody called the police.

The police officers dispersed the party and put several of the noisiest boys, including Josef and one of his close friends, into their police cars. The police drove for a short time and then stopped at Tuřany, kicked the boys out, gave them a few slaps, and let them walk home. Josef´s friend, probably the noisiest one, did not return home, fearing that the police might come again to his parents' house to arrest him. He settled in the attic of Josef´s parents' house and decided to leave the country for the West. However, he didn't know how to go about it. There were rumors about people being shot at the border. These rumours were partly true, but probably exaggerated and spread by the communists as propaganda to scare timid, submissive people.

Josef asked if I could help him. He wanted to introduce the young man to me, but I refused to see him. The fewer people I knew the better, and the less dangerous. I shared with Josef the information I had acquired from Commander Spáčil.

I didn't know at that time if Josef's friend had successfully escaped. I met Josef forty years later in 1990. He told me that his friend succeeded in reaching Austria by following my instructions. I heard that he became a professor in Alaska. I never met him.

13. Rajhrad

THE TOWN OF RAJHRAD TOOK ITS NAME FROM AN eleventh century Benedictine monastery. Hrad means fortress. A prince gave an abandoned fortress to the Benedictine monks who then transformed it into a monastery. A village bearing the same name developed around the resident monks.

The Mother House of religious sisters named Těšitelky (Consolers of the Sacred Heart of Jesus) is also in Rajhrad. I was sent by Felix to this house. From Pavlov where Felix was hiding, I went to Chrlice and stayed for a few days with an older lady named Johanka who knew me from childhood. My parents had already relocated to Nedašov. In Chrlice I depended on my old friends. I borrowed a bicycle and rode to Rajhrad. I had no idea that I was riding on a dangerous road.

The road to Rebešovice, a small village between Chrlice and Rajhrad, was lined on both sides with cherry trees about thirty metres apart. A man was standing beside every second or third tree. It dawned on me that these men were secret police officers. Any one of them could stop me and demand the personal documentation that every citizen was required to have with him at all times. When I realized my precarious position, I quickly turned off the main road onto the dusty side roads. I arrived at the Těšitelky's Mother House from the rear. I located the main entrance and asked for Mother Marta, the Abbess.

After a short while, a woman in religious habit came to the guest room where I was waiting. She seemed to be about fifty years old. I introduced myself and explained why I was there. With a smile, she said that we would talk after I ate lunch. She confirmed that indeed the road was guarded by police because a Hungarian communist government delegation was travelling the road on the way to Prague. She asked a sister to bring me lunch, and then she left.

After I finished my lunch, Mother Marta returned with a young man of about thirty years of age who had a communist red star on his lapel. She introduced him as Father Šicner who would be part of our refugee group. She also informed me that there was another priest, a Jesuit, hiding in the bee house in their garden, and asked me whether I wanted to meet him. I declined. If I were arrested, the fewer people I knew the better. She didn't ask any questions about Felix or why I had come. She was well informed. She knew Felix personally and knew about his current situation through one of her sisters who was from Horní Štěpánov.

Mother Marta explained that she had started the illegal operation of helping people escape from Czechoslovakia after the communists had prevented her sisters from going to one of their religious houses in Argentina. Only a handful of sisters knew what their Mother House was secretly doing. The rest of the community knew nothing about it.

Without wasting time on pleasantries, we got down to business. Mother Marta outlined the plan. On a certain date, two well armed Czech men would arrive at night from Vienna at a designated tree in the fields in the prohibited, guarded border zone. They would lead a group of ten refugees across the border and provide transportation to Vienna through the Soviet occupied zone. On the given date, the ten refugees would gather at a farmer's house in the village of Hrušky outside of the prohibited border zone. From there, Bohuš, a son of a farming family, would take command of the group and at night lead the refugees through the fields to a solitary tree in the prohibited zone. At that tree, the group would wait for the two armed men from Vienna. Felix's group was allowed to have three members out of ten.

The possibility of a shootout and people being captured or killed was real. Everyone had to take responsibility for himself, she explained. Each of us in the group had to pay 10,000 crowns for the service (the Czechoslovak currency of considerably less value than the Austrian shilling). The two men had expenses connected with their risky operation, like paying an Austrian truck driver for transporting us through the zone controlled by the Soviet Red Army.

I explained to Mother Marta that I was poor and had no money. She gave me 3,000 crowns. I returned to Johanka in Chrlice and never saw Reverend Mother Marta again.

14. Police Trap

Iᴏɴáᴄ ʙɪʟíᴋ, ᴀɴ ᴇʟᴇᴍᴇɴᴛᴀʀʏ ꜱᴄʜᴏᴏʟ ᴛᴇᴀᴄʜᴇʀ and a survivor of the infamous Nazi concentration camps, was a good friend to Felix and me. He arrived in Chrlice on Felix's motorcycle, searching for me.

"Where is Felix?" he asked when he found me. Ignác had gone first to Horní Štěpánov, and there somebody told him that he would find me in Chrlice. He told me that he had a reliable way to cross the border clandestinely with false documents. Several people had already made a safe crossing. I told him I knew where Felix was and I would inform Felix about the new escape plan. After I knew Felix's decision, I would contact Ignác at his home in Boršice.

I went to Pavlov to meet Felix. He decided to leave the country by the "safest way," which meant Ignác's plan. All my moving around the country was done by trains paid for by Felix, on a bicycle or on foot. I kept moving day and night without much sleep. From Pavlov I travelled to Boršice and relayed Felix´s decision to Ignác. He took me to the town of Nedakonice and introduced me to Stanislav Holáň, the owner of a general store. The next step was to get Felix from Pavlov to Stanislav´s home in Nedakonice.

Based on Stanislav's resourcefulness, and with Felix's agreement, I decided the best time to move Felix from Pavlov to Nedakonice would be the following Sunday. My task would be to drive with Stanislav to Pavlov, pick up Felix, and head to Chrlice where Vlasta would be waiting at his parents' home. With a little luck it would be easy to get him to Nedakonice.

On Sunday before noon, I arrived at Nedakonice, where Stanislav's wife served me lunch. Meanwhile, Stanislav was getting his car ready. When I saw what he was doing, it concerned me. With black paint, he was changing his car license numbers. When I questioned him, he said that if the authorities spotted us, they'd get the wrong license number. I told him that it was not a good idea because if the police stopped us with a license number not corresponding to the car documents, we would be in trouble. Stanislav agreed and washed the paint off the license plates.

Indeed, a police officer did stop us on our way to Pavlov and requested identification, but talked only to Stanislav. The police were in the village to deal with fighting and riots after a soccer game.

At Pavlov, we quickly squeezed Felix into the trunk of the car and drove away. When we were out of the danger area, we got Felix out of the trunk to ride with us. Stanislav was tired and didn't want to drive to Chrlice late at night. After a short discussion, all three of us agreed that I would go to Chrlice by train and meet Felix´s mother and Vlasta.

When I arrived at Davídek's house, it was already late at night. I told both women that Felix was safe and fine, but not able to come home to say goodbye to his family. Then I went to my friend Johanka's house where I slept for the night. She didn't know anything about what was taking place. As a good friend of mine, she trusted me and did not ask any questions.

It was left up to me to make decisions about which three friends would leave Czechoslovakia by the Rajhrad way, and who would have the opportunity to escape by the safest way. I wanted to use the safest way and go with Felix because I was afraid that if I were caught by the Rajhrad way, interrogated and incarcerated, I could get other people into trouble. Felix would not go without Vlasta. Josef Pluháček knew most people who protected Felix after his escape from the police station, so it was decided that Felix, Vlasta, Josef and I would go by the safest way. Three of Felix's friends and collaborators would go by the riskier Rajhrad way.

Vlasta returned from Chrlice to Horní Štěpánov with my message to Ladislav Vařeka that I wanted to meet him at the railroad station in Brno. Ladislav was one of Felix's brightest students and a good friend of mine. The other smart and adventurous fellow among Felix´s students was Stanislav Florián. Dr. Vladimír Richter definitely deserved the opportunity to leave Czechoslovakia because as a mathematician assisting his professor at the university, he also studied theology and was a good intellectual candidate for incarceration. His older brother, a Jesuit, was already in jail.

My first chosen man for the Rajhrad group was Vilém Juza, my close and reliable friend. He accepted my offer with enthusiasm and his father supported him. When I told Vilem that there were serious risks and the possibility of being shot and incarcerated, he changed his mind. Dr. Vladimír Richter accepted my offer. Ladislav Vařeka saved me without knowing it. I felt that I must be honest and tell him about the dangers on the Rajhrad way as I had told Vilém. Ladislav disappointed me because he decided to go the safest way with Felix and not the more dangerous way by Rajhrad. Since three of us could not go via the safe way, Ladislav's decision forced me to escape to Austria via Rajhrad.

On the same day that I was coordinating our illegal escape plans in Chrlice, Dr. Richter, Vilém and I received an order from the Czechoslovak army to gather in the Mimoň army barracks. To disobey that order meant facing the military tribunal. By coincidence, the date to be in Mimoň was the same date we were supposed to leave the country—the next day. We had to act immediately.

By then the police knew where Felix was. The safe way group was gathering around Felix at the Holáňs' home in Nedakonice. The police continued to play ignorant in order to snare as many people as they could. We didn't know anything about the police involvement in our affairs. The consequences for Felix and his friends were tragic.

I met with Laďa Vařéka forty years later in 1990. He told me that the key organizer of the safe way testified in court as a witness wearing a high ranking police uniform.

Felix was sentenced to twenty-four years in prison, Josef Pluháček to six, Láďa and Josef Hampl to three; Stanislav Holáň, Ignác Bilík, and a miller were each given several years in prison. For Ignác, it meant returning to a concentration camp, only this time to a Czechoslovak camp instead of a German camp. Seventeen-year-old Vlasta was sentenced to one and a half years in prison, including six months in solitary confinement.

According to communist jurisprudence, they were all criminals. They did not steal, they did not kill—they did something much worse. By their activities, they were undermining the victorious communist establishment by refusing to believe the Marxist-Leninist ideological creed.

III. REFUGEE AND IMMIGRANT

15. To Austria

IT WAS LATE AFTERNOON AT THE BRNO RAILROAD station when Ladislav Vařeka and I parted company with the words, "See you in Salzburg." I took an express train to the town of Brumov. From Brumov I caught a connecting train to Valašské Klobouky. It stopped briefly in Návojná. About one kilometre from there the train passed through a long tunnel on its way to Valašské Klobouky. From Návojná to my parent's home in Nedašov was about a twenty-five-minute walk.

Before leaving my country, I decided to return home to get some personal documents, pack a small suitcase with the basic necessities, and say goodbye to my family. The next morning at seven o'clock I had to be in Hrušky, located just outside the guarded border zone. Mother Marta had instructed me to be there before everyone else so that I could tell Bohuš and his family that a group of refugees would be gathering at their house. Otherwise there was a danger that the Bohuš' family might call police, assuming that a trap was being set up for them by the police themselves.

I was tired and sleepy, so I slept on the train from Brno to Brumov. In Brumov I woke up just in time to get to my connector train and then I fell asleep again. When I opened my eyes, the train was just departing from Návojná. I was shocked and panicked for a few seconds. Now what? The next possible connection wouldn't be until ten o'clock the next morning—too late!

"Now what, my guardian angel?"

I received an immediate answer. "You are in the first car of the train where the engineer is located. Run to him and ask him to stop the train immediately." And so I did. The driver stopped the train just at the entrance to the tunnel. I was relieved and energized. Happily, I walked through the plowed fields to my parents' house.

It was midnight. I was not expected, so naturally I woke everybody. I requested two favours from my family: not to ask me any questions, and to remember the name Mimoň. If anybody asked for me, they should tell them I went to Mimoň. I also asked my parents to wake me at five in the morning so I could catch the early train from Návojná to Brumov, and from there another train to Znojmo.

I had a strange and pleasant experience during the night. I awoke fully from my sleep with the feeling that somebody was standing by my bed and lovingly looking at me. It was an older woman. I thought at first that it was my mother who was sleeping in another bed in the same room, but soon I realized that the person standing at my bed was not my mother because I heard my mother breathing in her bed. To make sure that I wasn't mistaken, I addressed the lady with our customary word "Mami (Mother)." The lady quietly turned around and walked into the corner of the room and disappeared. The only light in the dark room was the natural light coming from the window. I was not disturbed; I felt peaceful and fell into a deep sleep again. To this day I do not know what the paranormal incident was about.

As instructed, at 5:00 a.m. my parents woke me up and the family gathered around. I reminded them not to ask any questions and not to forget the name Mimoň. I told them that I might be away for several years. After breakfast as I was departing, my father said that he wanted to walk with me to the railroad station. Of course I had no objections.

It was a beautiful, cool morning; the new day was dawning. As I entered the railroad car, my father reached up, shook my hand, and gave me a Czech-German pocket dictionary.

"Take it," he said. "You will need it."

That was the last time I ever saw him. He died as a result of a strong emotional shock caused by the invading Warsaw Pact armies under the Soviet Red Army command in 1968. He was alone at home while my mother was in Slovakia visiting my youngest brother

Peter whose wife was having their first baby. When my father heard shooting, he thought the war had started again.

I arrived at Hrušky at 7:00 a.m. and easily found Bohuš's family house. Bohuš was not home, but his sister knew the plan and invited me in. Bohuš came later with an illegal handgun in his pocket. Gradually the members of our refugee group assembled. By that afternoon all ten of us were ready to depart, but we had to wait until dark. Late in the evening we ran into the open fields following Bohuš. I was the last one, the poorest runner because of the childhood injury to my left leg, but I made it.

Once we were out of the village and in the fields, we slowed to a walk. After we crossed a road in the prohibited border zone, we found a young man waiting for us. He had a bicycle, a small demijohn with wine, and he smelled of alcohol. He reported to Bohuš that the guides from Austria could not make it. His home was in the prohibited zone and the border guards knew him. He told us that they had stopped him and thought that he was drunk as usual, which was not the case. They let him go. The group had to return to Hrušky and wait for two more days, he said. Bohuš could not accommodate all ten of us overnight. The young man with the demijohn had to take two of us with him to the town of Lanžhot, which was in the prohibited border zone. Nobody seemed willing to go; they wanted to return to Hrušky. I volunteered and Dr. Richter joined me.

The cloudy darkness was upon us. Vladimír and I were in the open fields, not knowing where we were being led. We were dependent entirely on the young man with the small demijohn. He led us to a group of houses on the outskirts of the town. He brought us to a house in the middle of those houses. There a young woman took us in.

Maria was a painter living alone in the house; she was a woman dedicated to beauty in art and prayer. Her house was decorated with Moravian Slovak cultural motifs. Our guide departed; Maria fed us and then we climbed a ladder to her attic. There in the hay Vladimír and I slept while army officers in Mimoň searched for us among the theology students. I learned about it only in 1990 from a theology student who was there and who knew Dr. Richter and me. During the day, Maria brought food up to the attic.

On the second night, just after midnight, two armed men moved into the attic. They did not say a word to us. They settled in the hay on the opposite side of the attic. The name of the leader was Franta. He was a married man with four children. He'd taken his family to a refugee camp in Austria after the communists had labelled him a capitalist and confiscated all of his property. Franta had been in the auto repair business in Lanžhot. He offered his services as a patriot to the American secret service located in Vienna. His spy work was his revenge against the communists. The Americans accepted him and armed him. He was moving back and forth between

Czechoslovakia and Austria through the Soviet occupied zone. In moving from Czechoslovakia to Austria, he took a group of refugees screened by Mother Marta in Rajhrad. He also had an associate who worked for the French secret service. They worked together as a team. Both of them knew the border terrain and also the movements of the border guards. Franta moved first in the darkness, his associate following him at a short distance covering his back.

On the third night just after ten o'clock, we descended from the attic ready to go. Close to Maria's house was a street light. Maria went out first, inspected the surroundings, and then signaled that the way was clear. Franta moved first and fast under the light, running into the darkness of the fields with his associate behind him. Vladimír Richter and I followed them. When we were far enough from the light in the dark fields, we stopped briefly in order to catch our breath, and then we continued following Franta.

The night was dark and cloudy, no stars to be seen. Visibility was almost zero. We approached the solitary tree in the field. Franta stopped us and went on ahead towards the tree. There he called a code word into the darkness; from the darkness came the voice of Bohuš with the answer. We moved toward the tree where the rest of our group was waiting. Franta's instruction was brief and clear: "Now you are under my command. There will be silence, no talk. There might be a communist agent among you. When necessary, you will hold hands, forming a chain because on occasion there will be no visibility and I don´t want to lose anyone. If anyone steps out of line or disobeys my orders, I will shoot him at once. Let's go!" I felt confident that we were in the hands of a good leader. We went on in silence.

At one point we were ordered to stop and lie on our bellies and wait until two border guards passed. We crawled under some wires. When we moved through a bush area, we formed a chain holding hands because it was so dark that it was almost impossible to see the person ahead. I was the last one in the chain, depending on the others. I didn't like it because if the chain broke, I would be lost. The only consolation I had was that if I made it, everybody made it.

We eventually arrived at the Dyje River which formed the border between Czechoslovakia and Austria. Before we entered the river, Franta instructed us: "Here the river is shallow. The water will be above your knees or maybe up to your waist. We have to move fast. After we cross the river, we'll be on the Austrian side. That doesn't mean that we'll be out of danger. As soon as we are out of the water, we must run to the huge straw stack. There everyone has to lean against the stack and not move! If you move around the stack, your silhouettes will be visible not only to the Austrian border guards, but also to the Czech guards. We will wait there for about an hour for a truck that will take us to Vienna."

After about an hour, a truck appeared on the road not far away from the haystack. It dimmed its lights three times and then turned them off and stopped. All twelve of us ran toward the big truck. The driver opened the back of the truck which was covered with canvas, and quickly removed empty vegetable boxes. Eleven of us disappeared into the back of the truck. The driver and Franta replaced the empty boxes, hiding us behind them. We then drove into the night.

The truck stopped suddenly and we heard Russian mixed with German. A Red Army patrol had stopped us. I hoped that Franta with his automatic folded assault rifle under his jacket would not lose his nerve and start shooting. He kept cool and co-operated when the Russian soldiers ordered them out of the truck. They opened the canvas of the truck and started to remove the empty boxes. I stopped breathing; I'm sure everyone else did too. After the soldiers were satisfied, they allowed us to proceed.

We arrived in Vienna early in the morning, just as the day was dawning. It was chilly. The truck stopped and we were herded into the open door of a building.

I learned that Franta was later betrayed and ambushed by police officers waiting for him at the fatal tree. When he called his secret code, rockets exploded in the air and lit the landscape with artificial lights hanging on little parachutes. During a brief shootout, Franta was hit in the stomach by several bullets. When he realized that he could not escape, he put a bullet through his head.

They did not capture him alive; his associate escaped to Vienna and reported the incident. I met Franta's widow and four children in a refugee camp in the American zone in Austria. The Americans accepted her shortly afterwards and took her to the U.S.A. I heard about her again when I was in Chicago about fifteen years later.

And what about Maria and Mother Marta? One of the refugees was a Benedictine priest. He told his mother everything he knew about the underground operation originating in Rajhrad. The mother, after she learned that her son was safely in Italy, told her neighbours how the wonderful sisters in Rajhrad had saved her son. The husband of one of the neighbours was a police officer. For such valuable information, he received a rich reward.

The Rajhrad underground operation was destroyed. Bohuš managed to save himself and eventually immigrated to Australia. Mother Marta and Maria were imprisoned for many years in a basement dungeon in Znojmo in almost complete darkness. It was hell for them, living in filth, lice and fleas. When I met Maria in the early 1990s at her house, she was a worn out old woman with a strong, unbroken character. She told me her story. Also, she confirmed the details of Franta's last minutes in this world. The story was corroborated by the police officers who participated in the ambush.

Of the many refugees she helped, Maria told me I was the only one who came to thank her. I wrote an article about her and published it in a Chicago Czech paper. When I visited Maria again two years later, she told me that a family in Australia had read my article and came to thank her. Where were the many other people who gained their freedom through her house? So much for human gratitude!

Maria is now dead. I don't know Mother Marta's fate, but I do know that both women were holy women of prayer and courage dedicated to the Church. The mother house in Rajhrad was expropriated by the communists and seriously damaged by their army. The house was returned to the sisters after the collapse of the Soviet empire.

The communist ideal of one world government is as alive today as it ever was, except it is no longer exclusive to communism. Some Christians believe in the idea of one religious world government. The idea of one world government seems to make sense to them. However, man's self-centred nature drives him to use his intelligence for selfish purposes in the guise of noble ideals.

I believe that all the unnecessary deaths and suffering of innocent people were not in vain. They have a super-rational value and power.

16. Vienna to Salzburg

THREE MEMBERS OF OUR REFUGEE GROUP LEFT US in Vienna. The rest of us, two priests and five seminarians, were immediately sent to the Vienna seminary. The students of the seminary were still on vacation. When we arrived at the seminary, we showered and had breakfast. For the main meal of the day, we were sent to the Vatican refugee services. Everyone had to sign a statement that he had received a well prepared, satisfying meal. We signed and lined up for the meal. It was served on clean plates in a clean setting; however, the amount of food on the plate could be placed on one soup spoon. That was it. We were hungrier after the "dinner" than before. It was cruel.

Since everyone in our group belonged to the clergy, we were treated better than the other refugees. Dr. Vladimír Richter and I were sent to the religious congregation of the Piarists Fathers where we received our meals and room free of charge. Where the other members of our group ended up I do not remember. Vladimír, who spoke German fluently, contacted the Jesuits in Vienna and applied for admission into their novitiate.

A few days later the Jesuits invited us for a spaghetti supper and offered to help us cross the Soviet occupied part of Austria to the American controlled city of Salzburg. All we had to do was wait. Meanwhile, I was learning German as quickly as I could.

After three weeks of waiting, the Jesuits bought us bus tickets and instructed us to travel to Gratz, but to get off the bus in a town before the border of the Soviet occupied zone. We were told to keep silent on the bus. When we got to that town, we were instructed to hide in the local Catholic church without speaking to the parish priest. He shouldn't know anything about what was taking place because he might be afraid that we were a Soviet trap. In the church, we should wait until a nun arrived to say her prayers. When she left, we should follow her at a distance. At a certain point, she would signal with her hand the direction we should run because that section of the Soviet occupied border zone was free from Soviet military patrols.

We waited about an hour in the church before the nun appeared. She briefly prayed and left. We followed her at a distance, and then she waved her hand and continued walking. We ran in the indicated direction down a hill without stopping. Again, I was the slowest, the last one.

We entered the British controlled territory and were finally free. We were so happy that it didn't bother us that we didn't know exactly where we were. We celebrated our escape by eating fresh plums that Father Burian had bought at a store.

We kept walking and tried to get oriented. It was evening. We reached the outskirts of a large town. Night was setting in; we didn't know where or how we would spend it. Father Burian, a survivor of the Nazi concentration camps and fluent in German, assumed the leadership of our group.

We found a religious house of nuns with the hope that they might accommodate us for the night. Father Burian rang the doorbell and a nun appeared. She warmly welcomed us. Then without any questions, she and another nun led us to individual rooms. I washed, undressed and crawled into a soft bed. It was hard to believe what was happening, but I was grateful for everything. I wondered about the miracle that was taking place.

I was almost asleep when I heard a loud order: "Heraus! Heraus!" (Out! Out!). A nun opened my door. I jumped out of bed and put on my pants, wondering what was going on. When I entered the corridor, there was a gathering of the rest of our refugee group. We were led downstairs to a large, cold basement storage room. Bewildered, we spent the rest of the night on beds without mattresses.

Early in the morning we were fed a modest breakfast and sent on our way to Salzburg through the territory controlled by the allied armies.

What happened that night? Why were we accepted so warmly without questions? The nuns had been expecting a group of seven seminarians who had reserved overnight accommodations with them. The students were delayed and had arrived an hour after us with apologies and explanations for why they were so late. The nuns realized their mistake and had to deal with the emergency they had created for themselves. They kept their real guests waiting somewhere in the building while several nuns got us out of our beds and quickly put the rooms back in order.

The improvised basement accommodations for the night were appreciated under the circumstances. Without the mix up, we probably wouldn't have been admitted. I am laughing as I write this. That night I was not laughing.

17. Salzburg

IN SALZBURG WE CONTACTED FATHER OMASTA, AN old friend of Burian and also of Felix. I had met Father Omasta almost two years earlier in Horní Štěpánov when he came to visit Felix. He recognized me at once. He knew Burian well from the Brno diocese. Omasta had escaped from Czechoslovakia more than a year earlier. He went first to Franco's Spain as a priest and worked among the poor. His mission there did not last long. He was accused in church circles of being a communist for paying too much attention to the poor. That accusation was too dangerous in Franco's fascist state. Eventually he left Spain and settled in Austria. Since he spoke German fluently, he was assigned by the Roman Catholic Diocese of Salzburg as a chaplain to a high school run by nuns. He connected Stanislav, Vladimír and me with Father Pitrun[5]. Together they took care of us refugee clerics.

When I told Father Pitrun about my encounter with Mr. Mikmek in Konice, we became friends. Father Pitrun resided with the Benedictines at Maria Plain Monastery on the outskirts of Salzburg where he was an organist. At the same time, he was a pastor for the Czech refugees living in a nearby refugee camp waiting to immigrate overseas.

Father Pitrun contacted Monsignor Berg, the rector of the seminary in Salzburg, an intelligent, compassionate man, a choir master, and later the Archbishop of Salzburg. Monsignor Berg accepted Vladimír and me into the Salzburg seminary. There I shared a room with two Austrian seminarians. Dr. Richter had his own room. He only spent a short time in the seminary, because the Jesuits soon called him into their novitiate. For Stanislav Florian, Father Pitrun arranged a modest, private room at the entrance to an old Salzburg monastery downtown. Two members of our group departed for Nepomucenum in Rome without wasting time in Salzburg. Father Burian stayed briefly with Stanislav and then disappeared. I learned that for some unknown reasons, he returned to Czechoslovakia the same way he left it. There he was arrested and died in prison. Our refugee group of ten disbanded.

In the Salzburg seminary there was another Czech refugee seminarian named Vladislav Urban. He was in fourth year theology and was preparing for deaconate and priestly ordination. He welcomed Stan and me. Unfortunately, because my German was poor, I didn't understand many of the lectures at the Faculty of Theology.

We were hungry and cold most of the time. Occasionally, Father Omasta took us three seminarians for a beer at a busy cellar at a local brewery. As refugees we had to submit to different interviews by separate officials—British, French and Austrian—in order to receive political refugee status, and with it an IRO (International Refugee Organization) one-way travel passport.

In spite of everything turning out so well, I felt uncomfortable about the political Cold War climate. Stalin was alive and dangerous. There was fear that his Red Army, with its communist Warsaw Pact allies, would sweep through the rest of Europe at any time. What held Stalin back were the American atomic bombs and the presence of the American army in Europe. The American soldiers could be seen maneuvering along the river Salzach. The noise of the low flying fighter jets over the city was impossible to ignore.

I didn't want to be caught in a sudden open war of East against West, or be caught in World War III. I was ready to join the Czechoslovak army organized from Czech and Slovak refugees living outside of Czechoslovakia. Such an army did not exist yet, but was being planned overseas, mainly in Canada and the United States.

I decided to immigrate somewhere overseas and enter a priestly seminary in the new country. Stanislav and Vláďa Urban decided to immigrate with me.

The United States contingent of political refugees was closed for us. Their quotas were full. The International Refugees Organization (IRO) offered us three other options: Canada, Australia and Venezuela. Somehow we got the message that in the eyes of the Canadian

Consulate at that time, if you were of Slavic origin, you were inferior and therefore only good for manual labour in mines, forests or on farms.

We dropped the Canadian option and decided between Australia and Venezuela by flipping a coin. Venezuela came up and so to Venezuela we went. I planned to enter the priestly seminary in Caracas, but not as a beggar. I would first find a way to put some money in my pocket. I was tired of being poor.

18. General Taylor Military Ship

FOLLOWING THE DIRECTIONS OF THE VENEZUELAN Consulate, Vláďa Urban, Stanislav Florián, and I boarded a special immigrant train in Salzburg destined for Bremen Hafen, Germany. As the train was approaching the harbour, which was not yet visible, I could smell the sea. A powerful, pleasant feeling overwhelmed me. "Finally home!" That was the enthusiastic, silent message emerging from my heart. As a boy, I loved water, creeks, rivers and lakes. Growing up in the middle of Europe, I had never been to the sea.

The train stopped not far from the city. We were taken to Camp Grohn, a large German military barracks abandoned by the German Wehrmacht army and now under the command of former soldiers of the Polish army. Many immigrants were already waiting there for ships to take them to different countries. Our trio had to wait three weeks for an American military ship named *General Taylor*. During the war it took soldiers to Germany. On its way back to the United States it took immigrants.

The Bremen Hafen weather was cloudy, humid and chilly. As young men, we were assigned to bunk beds in the attic of the barracks, each one of us with only one blanket. It was hard to get a good sleep because of the cold, but the food was good. There was nothing to do except walk around and wait.

Finally the day came when the three of us, together with many other men, women and children, boarded our ship. The boat was built for about two thousand soldiers. There were at least a thousand immigrants on board in my estimation. Most passengers were destined for the United States, but several hundred of us were going to Venezuela. The ship would sail to Venezuela and then the remainder of the immigrants would continue to the United States.

The ship's crew was reduced because its command counted on the help of the passengers, soldiers on their way to Germany, or able bodies like Stanislav and me heading the opposite direction. Our main tasks were in the dining hall, scraping the old grey paint from the rusting parts of the boat exposed to sea water and then repainting them. Of course, we could not work outside during stormy days.

The weather was rough. For three days and nights it was stormy. Sleeping in my bunk bed felt like living in an elevator moving up and down, day and night. Thirty feet up and then immediately thirty feet down. No wonder almost everyone was seasick and vomiting, some of the crew included, except for a few of us. Stanislav was ill, but still able to work. Vláďa Urban succumbed to the sea sickness and was good for nothing.

Everything was an adventure for me, satisfying my curiosity. I loved it all and volunteered for any kind of work. My permanent job was serving tea and distributing oranges in the dining hall and helping with the cleaning. Stanislav was a permanent hall cleaner. There were other tasks connected with the kitchen and the dining area that allowed me to see different parts of the ship, particularly its deep bowels and the food storage, accessible only by elevators. I was impressed with the rows of pig and cow carcasses hanging frozen in storage.

On stormy days I worked up to sixteen hours. The dining area was a mess during those days—mess on the tables and mess on the floor. Spilled and vomited food was everywhere, moving and flowing on the floor from one end of the dining area to the other, back and forth, according to the up and down motion of the ship in the huge waves. Collecting the mess with large shovels and putting it into the barrels sliding there and back on the slippery floor was quite a bit of fun ... at least for young men like us.

People were encouraged to eat in order to ease their stomach cramps, but few followed the advice. Many did not eat and felt like dying. The waters were much calmer when we sailed into the tropical Caribbean Sea.

One morning after more than ten days at sea, pas- sengers became excited. There was distant land on the horizon and everybody wanted to see it. A little later the ship stopped. We were in Venezuelan waters and needed permission to land. After a few hours, a boat arrived and Venezuelan officers boarded our ship. Then we resumed our trip. When we arrived at Puerto Cabello, buses were waiting for us. We boarded the buses showing our IRO passports. They took us to El Trompillo, a camp run by two middle-aged Germans.

19. El Trompillo and Caracas

WHILE WAITING AT EL TROMPILLO FOR THREE weeks, I learned some interesting history about the camp. It was originally part of a successful coffee plantation privately owned by a German family. The family supported German submarines that operated in the Caribbean Sea during the war. In 1945, all the members of the family were murdered and the camp became the property of the government. How much of this story is true I don't know, but probably most of it is.

On Sundays when I lived in Caracas, my friends and I would travel by bus to La Quira's beautiful beaches. Four German submarines were anchored in the harbour, rusting in the sea water. I met a few friendly crew members from those boats. Some of these young men believed that Hitler was still alive and were expecting orders to go to war again. Such was their dedication.

One of the crew members, an older cook, invited me for a "Knoedl Mahlzeit," which is a dumpling supper. In his modest apartment on a military case, were two crossed femur bones with a skull in the middle and a capital letter V for victory. Below them was written: "Sieg oder Tod!" Victory or death! But my chef friend was an ordinary, pleasant fellow. Some of those young men were members of the famous SS troops.

The two German administrators of the El Trompillo camp sorted and organized the immigrants according to their skills or lack of skills. They were sending them to various parts of the country, mostly to Caracas. I thought they were fair and doing a good job. After about three weeks in the camp, they assigned me to another immigrant camp in Caracas because of my bookbinding skills. There I had food and a bed guaranteed for two weeks. Within fourteen days, I was expected to find employment to support myself. I was eager to find work, because I wanted to have money in my pocket before entering the seminary.

Every day for two weeks I went to businesses where I saw a possibility of employment, and I repeated a phrase that I'd learned from a small German-Spanish handbook: "Trobo travajo." The standard answer to my request was, "Maňana," which I thought meant "tomorrow," according to the dictionary. Strangely enough, the verb "trobar" did not exist in my small Czech-Spanish dictionary. The next day I returned to the same door where they had told me "Maňana," and was surprised when the door was slammed in my face.

Later I learned that the text in the German-Spanish handbook didn't make much sense. The proper phrase I should have used was "Busco travajo," which means, "I am searching for a job." The word "maňana" (tomorrow) has several meanings depending on the circumstances in which it's used. One meaning is "Go to hell." On top of it all, the verb "trobo," from the infinitive "trobar" was not Spanish but Catalan. In Catalan it meant "I have found a job." Such was my experience in learning Spanish.

At the end of the second week, with the help of a Czech immigrant who had settled in the city, I found a job at Editorial Ancora taking out garbage and cleaning the filthy toilet. My income was just sufficient for bread, milk, bananas, and simple accommodations. I knew that I was in the right place because by looking around, I realized that my bookbindery skills were better than any of the employees. It was only a matter of time. As soon as I learned enough Spanish and had an opportunity to show what I could do, I would be one of the top employees. Indeed, in less than a year I was a valued, respected and well paid worker.

Once I had saved some money, I applied for admission to the Caracas seminary. I gave my Maturity Certificate from the Gymnasium in Brno to the rector and was told to wait. The seminary would call me. I waited for a week and then went to see the rector. I was told the rector wasn't in. I returned again, but was told to wait. The rector was never at home when I came. I realized that he did not want to see me, and that the Jesuit novice in charge of the seminary entrance was not telling me the truth. I was disgusted! I wanted to get my Maturity Certificate from the rector, but there was no way to meet him. He was never home when I called. I couldn't believe it. The document was important to me. The door-keeper was obviously instructed by the rector what to tell me whenever I showed up.

I decided to set a trap for him. I took my friend Pavel, with me and asked him to wait outside the seminary. Then I went inside, met the door-keeping novice, and asked for the rector. I received the usual answer that he was not home. I thanked him and left. A while later I asked Pavel to ask for Father Rector. Pavel asked for the rector who immediately appeared at the door. When I saw the rector, I stepped forward and asked him to return my document. Without a word he left and returned with my Maturity Certificate. It was clear to me that I was not wanted.

My two friends Vláďa and Stanislav were sent by the two managers of the El Trompillo camp to Maracaibo, about a thousand kilometres to the west. They were given the necessary money for the trip. Instead of going to Maracaibo, however, they went to Caracas. As former seminarians in Caracas, they went straight to the seminary and were accepted there. When they had learned Spanish well enough, they left. Naturally, the rector of the seminary became suspicious of another Czech like me applying for admission. In retrospect, I realize that it was fortunate that I was not admitted.

20. Temptations

THE INTRIGUING SPANISH COLONIAL ATMOSPHERE and lifestyle were still evident and strong in Caracas in 1951. I found inexpensive accommodations with breakfast included at a pension. I lived there for a while with Franta Zeman and his friend, Jenda. Franta was a natural leader and an organizer, a generous and courageous idealist. With his good heart, he spontaneously looked after Czech immigrants, including me. He was making good money as a building contractor in the city.

One evening, three young Czech men arrived for a visit. They came from far away Maracaibo, where they were trying to find employment. In our friendly discussion about news and opinions, Franta, a faithful, practicing Roman Catholic, brought up the subject of faith and religion. The discussion became heated. Franta argued with Vlasta Jelínek, who claimed to be an atheist. Vlasta was a skillful, intelligent auto mechanic from Prague. I listened to the ongoing debate, but did not say a word.

After the three fellows left, Franta asked why I hadn't supported him in the discussion. I explained that I had nothing to contribute because Vlasta had a more gracious image of God than my believing friends.

Several weeks later by coincidence, I met Vlasta on Avenida Petaré. He asked me the same question about why I hadn't entered into the discussion about faith and religion.

"Because you knew more about God than our friends who were trying to convince you about God's existence," I replied. There on the sidewalk, Vlasta described an understanding of God that was thoughtful and beautiful.

"If there was such a God, and He was the one who created the mess in which we are living in this world, I would spit in His face. Look, right here on this avenida. Not long ago, there was some sort of church parade sponsored by the government. It was an expensive undertaking and a waste of money. Two blocks below this avenida there is poverty, misery, and suffering. No! I don't want to have anything to do with such a God or with your church!"

"There is much more to it," I replied. "It's not so simple; your story is not the whole story."

After working for a few months performing ruling tasks at Ediorial Ancora, Mr. Matiz, the owner, started to appreciate me. He assigned me to tasks that other employees couldn't handle and he raised my salary. He invited me to become a member of the Millonarios de Caracas soccer team, as he was on the board of directors. On the soccer field I played defense. I was still a poor runner, but I compensated with my aggressiveness.

During my time in Caracas, two younger German Benedictine monks left the monastery and met with my ex-seminarian friends Stanislav and Vláďa. I never met the two ex-monks, but according to them, I should leave Venezuela if I was serious about becoming a priest. As an immigrant secular priest, I would be assigned to some diocese deep in the interior where priests don't want to go. After my ordination, I would be taken there by a government plane without a chance of easily coming back to the civilized world. To my knowledge, in the early 1950s, Venezuela was sparsely populated, with only about five million inhabitants.

The information from the two monks put me on alert. I went to see an older Slovak Salesian priest who had been a missionary in Venezuela for over twenty years. He confirmed the negative perceptions of the two former Benedictine monks. He told me that there was a significant difference between secular clergy and religious clergy. Religious clergy were looked after as missionaries by their order or congregation, while secular clergy were left to their bishops and their own ingenuity.

"What would you do," the missionary asked me, "if you came to a parish of natives as a white man and found a dilapidated baroque church, and in the rectory a young woman smoking a cigarette, waiting for you and telling you that she was your wife? Where would you turn? That girl might be the daughter of the most influential family in the community. If you did not accept her, you would be socially finished there. For you as a secular priest, it would be difficult to leave. You would not be able to expect much help from your bishop. He would have more pressing problems."

After my failed attempts to enter the Caracas seminary, I asked a friend who knew English to write an application letter for me to the Oblates of Mary Immaculate congregation in Saskatoon, Canada. That seemed to be the only alternative ... except for Rome which was a long shot according to Felix. I received a positive reply from the Oblates with instructions to wait. I waited for over a year without hearing from them. During that time I focused on saving money for my future studies.

I knew a Czech man, Alois Štěpán,[6] who was a border guard in Czechoslovakia, a military man who had no other skills but military discipline and handling of weapons. He had left his country in an emergency situation when it was discovered that he was helping people escape from the communists. His wife and children remained behind. He spoke often about his wife and family, saying that he would send for them after the expected war was over. If war started, he would fight on the front lines. He was a good, trusting, industrious man, and a friend of mine. In Caracas he supported himself by operating washing machines in a small laundry.

I suggested that he and I start our own laundry business. I would invest my money in this venture, and then after it became profitable, he could take over and gradually pay me back with interest. I could use that money for my future studies. He liked the idea, so we became partners.

I left my bookbindery employment at Editorial Ancora and started a laundry business with Alois. We hired four local women whom I had to train. It was a learning experience for me. In the beginning, I had to concentrate on building a clientele and keeping our small business afloat. No profit was possible. Alois and I were working gratis, just for food and two bunk beds in the back of the laundry. At the end of each week, he saw that I had an impressive amount of money, but after I paid salaries and utilities, there was barely enough to survive.

"Where is the money?" Alois asked week after week. I explained the financial situation to him several times. An unpleasant tension gradually grew between us. Finally, I threatened to give the laundry to him and return to my former bookbindery job. He continued challenging me. We were getting angry with each other. In a nutshell, I had miscalculated. I had failed. He did not believe that I could find a job and thought I was bluffing. Finally, I told him that enough was enough. "Keep the laundry," I said. "I'll stay for two more weeks to teach you how to manage the business and then I'm gone." He still didn't believe that I would leave and find another job.

I went to see Mr. Montealegre, the owner of La Impresora firm in Caracas and explained that I wanted to work for him. As a friend of Mr. Matiz, he knew about me from Editorial Ancora. He asked me what salary I expected. When I said twenty-five bolivars a day, he replied that nobody at his factory of thirty-five employees was paid that much. I persisted with my salary demand, promising to return in two weeks.

Two German fellows were running Mr. Montealegre's factory as foremen. Their salary was twenty-two bolivars per day. When I arrived, I took over as foreman. When they learned about my salary, one of them quit at once. The other fellow and I collided soon after in the presence of the other workers. Mr. Montealegre was absent. The young fellow refused to do what I asked.

"You will not tell me what to do and how to do it," he stated.

It was obvious that my authority was being challenged because I was new. If I backed down, my authority would be undermined with all the employees and he would dominate. A tense silence surrounded us as we faced each other. All the workers were watching to see what would happen. With clenched fists, this fellow was ready to jump me. He was a young man about my height. Trembling with fear, I grabbed a large wrench. I knew that if I hit him with the wrench, I could badly hurt him or even kill him.

The confrontation ended in my favour. The fellow backed down. Eventually he became my best and most co-operative worker when he realized that I knew more than he did and that I had authority over him.

Mr. Montealegre showed his trust in me by giving me the keys not only to the factory, but also to his car. He gave me authority over ordering materials, arranging for maintenance of all machinery, and making most work decisions without consulting him. He was happy with my reports and explanations. I was in a secure and financially sound position once again.

In the summer of 1953, the country celebrated national festivities to mark a statutory holiday. That meant four days of free time for me. I was living alone and occasionally I felt lonely. Four days of vacation with nothing to do was a long time, so I decided to explore the country outside of Caracas. I took a taxi to Maracaibo which was about a thousand kilometres away. It turned out to be a rewarding learning experience. Without air conditioning in the tropical summer, the taxi ride to Barguisimeto was hot. At Barguisimeto, I changed to another taxi. Shortly after leaving the city, the taxi driver started looking for a gas station. He left the main road and got lost among high cacti rooted in the sandy soil. We kept wandering among the cacti, not knowing where we were or how to get back to the main road. I was not disturbed -actually, I enjoyed it.

We stumbled upon a gutted goat carcass covered with flies hanging from a cactus plant. Its flesh was crawling with putrid larvae. It was a sign of a settlement nearby where we could get gas. The driver felt relieved and explained that the tropical sun in a few days would kill all the worms and dry out the meat, preserving it. Shortly after, we found the settlement where we bought gas and supper.

The sun quickly disappeared behind the horizon. In one of the huts of the settlement we ate a "typical" Venezuelan meal ... well, not typical for me. There was no electricity, so the "restaurant" hut was dark except for the light coming from the fireplace on the ground in a corner. The faces of the inhabitants were barely visible except for the whites of their eyes and their teeth. I was the only white man in the place.

The supper of potatoes, rice and a piece of a goat meat cooked together in water was tasteless. It was difficult for me to eat it, but I did. I remembered my mother's stories about the missionaries in Africa who had to eat snails and insects. Now it was my turn to eat the goat meat dried by the tropical sun with all the preserved larvae. I imagined there was nothing between the food and my stomach—no mouth, no throat, just the stomach into which the food from the table had to disappear.

Seeing the living conditions of the people, I empathized with them, but at the same time I felt afraid. However, they were good to us, sold us gas and directed us to oil pipes that we could follow to get back to the main road. Once back on the road, my driver became ill so I had to drive. I drove for awhile until he asked me to stop. He got out of the car and vomited his supper. Then he felt better and took over the wheel again. I digested it all.

We arrived in Maracaibo at about four in the morning. I asked the driver to take me to a hotel. There I rented a room with open windows and two fans running at full speed. It was very hot. When I stepped into the shower, I turned on the cold water tap and jumped away when hot water hit my body. There was no cold water. The local law required that public places have a water reservoir on the roof for fire emergencies. The tropical sun had heated the water almost to boiling, which was why there was no cold water.

Fatigued, I collapsed onto the comfortable bed to get some sleep. Suddenly, the door opened and a beautiful teenage girl entered, shyly announcing that she was there to sleep with me. That did not correspond to my ascetic ideals and practices, so I thanked her and sent her away. A few minutes later, there was a knock on my door. The manager, a woman in her thirties, asked me politely whether it was true that I had refused the young woman. I confirmed it; she left the room shaking her head and muttering something about what kind of a man I was.

The next morning I went out to see the city. A boat was anchored in the harbour; sailors with their white skin burned red from the tropical sun were unloading and loading cargo.

I had a strong urge to join them and travel the world. *That would be the end of my promise to do my best to become a priest,* I thought. The desire to join the sailors was only a temptation. I dropped the idea.

IV. BACK TO EUROPE

21.Italian FRANCA Passenger Boat

ONE BEAUTIFUL MORNING WHILE WALKING TO work through the streets of Caracas, I prayed, "What do you want from me, Lord? I have done what I could to enter a seminary and all for nothing."

I was twenty-four years old in 1953, the year Stalin died. I had a respectable job with a decent income. Nothing had come from my application to enter the Oblates in Canada. What was I supposed to do? Get married and start a family?

The doors to the priesthood seemed to be shut, except for one possibility ... Rome. In order to do my best to become a priest as I promised in the chapel before the Blessed Sacrament during the retreat in Brno in 1947, I had to explore the Rome possibility.

I decided to apply to the Czechoslovak Nepomucenum College in Rome. Then whichever door opened first, the Oblates in Canada or the Nepomucenum College in Rome, is where I would go. Otherwise, I would build my future as a lay person in Venezuela. I preferred the

Oblates in Canada, but I would go to Rome if Rome replied first. The next day I wrote to Rome.

Five weeks later, I received an answer from Monsignor Bezdíček, the vice-rector and disciplinarian at the Nepomucenum College: "You are accepted. Two students from Bishop Trochta´s seminary in Litoměřice escaped and are here. They know you and recommended you. Contact the Apostolic Nuntiatur in Caracas for further directions. The Apostolic Nuncius will assist you."

As a refugee, I couldn't get a Czechoslovak travel passport and I still didn't have Venezuelan citizenship. The assistance of the Nuncius was essential. Four days later I received a letter from the Oblates in Canada: "You are accepted. Arrange your travel through the Canadian Consulate in Caracas." Without further hesitation, I made an appointment with the Nuncius and forgot about Canada. The Canadian offer had come too late.

When I went to see the Nuncio, His Excellency Armando Lombardi, the Vatican diplomatic represen-tative in Venezuela, he kindly welcomed me. He was dressed in his reddish-purple bishop's cassock with a biretta on his head. We talked about the church situation, particularly in Venezuela. Tears were running down his cheeks. I was impressed because he—a much older, expe-rienced and knowledgeable diplomat—needed to confide in a young fellow like me. We talked for over an hour. I felt that he was human and lonely, and I empathized with him. Subsequently, without any problems, I obtained a one way Venezuelan passport.

I felt guilty when I told my employer Mr. Montealegre that I was leaving for Rome, even though he was kind and accepting. We went together to a Salesian church where we prayed and said goodbye. When I took over the foreman's job in his factory, he was looking for a larger facility because there was no longer enough space for his growing business. When I left the factory after six months, there was plenty of space because I had reorganized work procedures. Several large orders were delivered before their deadlines. They could not have been delivered with the previous layout. Also, I introduced new skills to his workers. I felt guilty for leaving, yet at the same time I felt that my priority was Rome.

When I applied for an Italian visa through an Italian travel agency, they wrote on my travel document that I was Protestant. Although I tried to explain that I was Roman Catholic going to study theology in Rome, my explanation was not accepted. I was told that I could not be a Roman Catholic because I wasn't an Italian, so I arrived in Rome as a Protestant.

In October, 1953, I travelled to Italy on the *Franca*, an old passenger boat. The sea was calm. I had an enjoyable time, except for feeling lonely. During the trip, I learned that the *Franca* was built before World War I. At the beginning of the war, it was used as a military ship for Italian troops, but it was sunk near the Canary Islands.

After the war, the Italians pulled it out of the water, rebuilt it and used it as a passenger boat again. During World War II, the same thing happened when the British sank it. The boat was rescued after the war, repaired, and used as a passenger boat again. It travelled between Venezuela and Curasao Island, as well the French colony islands in the Caribbean, and the Madeira Islands in the Azores. The ship stopped for several hours at each island and we were allowed to spend some time touring the harbour.

In Madeira, I was stopped by a Portuguese customs officer and told I was not allowed to leave the boat because I was born in Czechoslovakia and therefore must be a communist. I felt insulted, but the officer thought that he knew better. My explanations were useless. At the Canary Islands, we stopped at Santa Cruz where I got a haircut and a manicure. At the barber shop, I was politely asked if I desired a girl for half an hour.

When I returned to the *Franca*, a middle aged Muslim passenger who had befriended me during the voyage, told me that he was searching for me because he had connected with two nice girls with white skin—one for me and one for him. He told me that he had a great time with them.

We sailed along the coast of Africa, past Gibraltar, and stopped at Barcelona where I briefly visited the city. Moored in the harbour was a replica of Columbus' ship, the *Santa Maria*. I imagined the hardships the crew endured on their voyage across the Atlantic. We also passed by the Majorca Islands. I disembarked at Naples and took a train to Rome. The *Franca* continued to its mother port in Genoa.

When I rang the bell at the entrance of the Collegium Nepomucenum, it was after 10:00 p.m. Everybody seemed to be asleep. Father Tomko, who later became a curial Cardinal, opened the door and welcomed me. He impressed me as a young, friendly priest. After a light supper, he showed me to my room.

The next morning I met Monsignor Bezdíček, the vice-rector and the real boss at the college. Then I met Monsignor Bontempi, the official rector and head of the college. A meeting with my two old friends from the seminary in Litoměřice, George Engelhardt and Josef Hurton, followed. Later I met Father Tomáš Špidlík, S.J., the spiritual advisor at the college. He and I became good friends. We used to have discussions about spirituality and the church. Years later, he visited my wife and me in Canada on several occasions. As a writer, Father Špidlík published over one hundred spiritual books which were translated into many languages.

After I settled into the college, I gave Father Tomko all my money so I was poor again. There I was … dependent at the bottom of the heap, but it didn't bother me. I was finally where I wanted to be: in a cassock, a Roman collar on my neck, and a large black renaissance style hat on my head. It made me feel holy, but I knew there was a long road ahead toward true holiness. I was finally on the path to fulfilling the promise I had made in Brno six years earlier.

JIŘÍ (GEORGE) HOŘÁK

22. Rome

I SPENT ALMOST FIVE YEARS IN ROME WITHOUT leaving the city, except for a few trips with seminarians and superiors to visit significant historical and cultural places, and for summer vacations near Livorno.

The Nepomucenum College discipline was strict. Silence had to be observed at all times. Personal correspondence was censored by the vice-rector. To enter another student's room for a chat was prohibited. The rooms were equipped with a cold water tap with a basin, a kneeler, a table and chair, a bed and a closet. Hot water showers were available in the basement on Saturdays. The college was short of money and dependent mostly on American benefactors of Czech origin. The protector of the college was Cardinal Ottaviani, a former rector of the Collegium Bohemicum at the time when the Nepomucenum College was built and opened in 1929. From time to time, he visited us at the Nepomucenum.

Years later, working as a staff training officer for the Ontario Ministry of Correctional Services, I visited various jails and large correctional institutions. The rules and discipline in the correctional institutions were not much different than the discipline at Nepomucenum, except for one significant variation ... we were not behind bars. We were in the college because we had a living faith and wanted to be there. We could quit at any time, while prisoners with their resentment, anger or depression, are forced against their wills to be where they are. We could sing, joke and laugh—and we did.

We compared our situation with Polish theology students in Rome at that time. Their country was also under a communist regime, but it was a very different regime from the one in Czechoslovakia. They could return to Poland for their vacations and come back to Rome again. Their Cardinal Wojtyla could travel in the West and visit various Polish communities, while our Cardinal Beran was under house arrest and later forcibly exiled to Rome without being allowed to return to Prague. He died in exile.

The communist government in our native country hated us and was obviously afraid of our faith, enthusiasm and ideals. Occasionally photographers from the Czechoslovak foreign intelligence service stood at the main entrance to Nepomucenum taking pictures of us seminarians as we walked to school. Polish theology students did not have such an irritating, ridiculous annoyance.

Nepomucenum College was built for about sixty students. Being cut off from its homeland and from the Church in Czechoslovakia by the Nazis during the war and then by the communists, it was financially supported by a large community of foreign resident priests from around the world who had come to Rome to take a doctorate, usually in canon law. Many who resided at the Nepomucenum facilities paid for their accommodations. We, the Czech and Slovak seminarians, were prohibited from having any contact with them. Cooking and laundry were done by the small community of Sisters of Saint Carlo Boromeo; cleaning was done by an Italian young man who resided at the college. The sisters sacrificed their lives for the love of Christ and worked for the Church for almost nothing.

Surrounded by people of faith in action, I felt content and happy. They were my kind of people. It's true that we experienced frustrations. We loved the Church as it was, in spite of our frequent criticism of it. We believed in its revitalization and mission in the world, and hoped for reform in the not too distant future. Our negative emotions were resolved by devotions, music, songs and laughter. Our spiritual director Father Tomáš Špidlík, S.J., who had an understanding heart, a sense of humour and good counselling skills, was invaluable in our institutional setting.

The lectures at the Atheneum Lateranense were in Latin and Italian. Learning in these two languages was a struggle for me during the first year and, to some extent, later on too. The methods of teaching foreign languages were rather primitive compared to the methods available today. Talented people were good at it. I was not. I had to learn the hard way. I kept mixing my Spanish with Italian during the initial stage of my studies. After several years, I managed to speak Latin and Italian fluently, although not perfectly.

We spent our summer vacations in a villa near Livorno, about three hundred kilometres north of Rome. A few students from the United States who studied at Nepomucenum were an exception to the rule. They were allowed to go home, but had to be back in September. Our villa in the rural area near Livorno served as our recreation during the hot summer months. The cicadas never stopped their all-pervading noisy songs during the hot days.

Nobody was allowed to leave our large agricultural villa area surrounded by walls without permission. You had to be accompanied by another seminarian if you needed to see a doctor or a dentist. We had a lot of free time. Each week we would go as a group for a picnic to the forest in the surrounding hills. When we went to the sea, Andrew, a Slovak seminarian from Argentina, would often catch large octopuses. He caught them, but it was up to me to kill them. I always felt uncomfortable when the eye of the octopus looked at me. The next day we would have octopus lunch prepared by the sisters. There were many joyful activities and games during the summer months at the villa.

It was required at the Nepomucenum College that within the first year, a seminarian had to swear not to enter any religious order for at least five years after his priestly ordination. I started to play with the idea of entering the Capuchins, the Benedictines or the Jesuits. I was not interested in a career like monsignor or even bishop. To become a secular priest was good enough for me. At the time I thought that if I could become a religious to achieve a deeper and more focused spirituality, it would be superior.

I was interested in spirituality and was well understood by my spiritual director Father Špidlík, S.J. The proper thing to do would be to leave Nepomucenum and enter a novitiate; however, if I did that and then discovered that the religious order was not for me, then all doors to the priesthood would be closed. Monsignor Bezdíček warned me that if I left to enter a religious order and then changed my mind to return to Nepomucenum, he would never allow me back. He insisted that I must make the obligatory oath.

In evaluating my situation, I concluded that I must become a priest first and then apply for admission to a novitiate immediately after my ordination. I refused to commit myself to the five year waiting period. Monsignor Bezdíček insisted that I must leave if I did not swear the promise. I refused to leave. After putting so much effort into studying for the priesthood, I couldn't risk leaving Nepomucenum College without the option of being able to return. If they wanted me out of Nepomucenum, they would have to call the Carabinieri (Italian police), but I would not swear the promise to wait for five years.

Monsignor Bontempi, the rector, and Father Špidlík, became my protectors.

A year and a half later, Monsignor Bontempi approached me one afternoon to inform me that he could no longer protect me. I assumed Cardinal Ottaviani had been informed by Monsignor Bezdíček about my stubbornness. The good rector made a proposal to me: "The document of your oath must be sworn and filed at Cardinal Confalonieri's curial office. You can make the oath in a chapel in my presence only, and leave out all those words with which you disagree. However, you must sign the document as it stands and I will sign it as the witness. That way your conscience will be free. Otherwise, you must leave our college." Cardinal Confalonieri had authority over me because he represented our incarcerated and house arrested Czech and Slovak bishops.

I appreciated Monsignor Bontempi's generous offer and thanked him, but "Litera scripta manet" means a written document remains. Words are words and my words may not be believed in the future when I explain to the cardinal what really took place in the chapel—namely that the Latin document was not sworn as it stands.

I asked Monsignor Bontempi to give me a blank form of the oath so that I could study it in my room before we went to the chapel. Then I would swear on the Bible on the altar. He agreed to it. The good rector was suffering with a progressive form of diabetes and his sight was not very good. In my room, I took a ruler and a sharp pencil and crossed out all the words I did not want to swear. I did it so lightly that the lines were barely visible. And so I swore it, leaving out all words of my commitment to the five years, signed it and Monsignor Bontempi co-signed it. The document was filed with the Cardinal's office. Both of us were happy, and Monsignor Bezdíček was satisfied.

Monsignor Bezdíček had a good heart, but he was a hard sergeant major. He was from the old school, probably partly trained under Cardinal Ottaviani in the old Collegium Bohemicum. He spent most of his life within the clerical environment of Rome. To my knowledge, he had very little pastoral experience in a parish community or with laity in general, except for hearing confessions, mostly of devout Italian women.

After my second year of theology, I took a siesta at the summer villa of Livorno and had a significant experience in the form of an intense dream. In my dream, I saw a young, beautiful, black-haired woman who came to me and said, "I am your wife."

"No, you are not my wife and never will be," I replied. "I am going to be a priest."

"Oh, yes," she said, "I am your wife and I will live with you."

We began to argue back and forth. Although attractive, she was an impediment to my becoming a priest. I couldn't get rid of her. In the dream, I realized that I was sleeping and dreaming. I tried to wake up, but I could not. "I must wake up out of this," I repeated to myself as I put all my energy into waking up. I could not. She would not let me go. Finally, I said, "Show me your face so that I can recognize you when you appear in my life." She turned her face towards me and all I saw were blank feminine cheeks ... no eyes, no nose, no mouth ... only black hair around her blank face. "Give me your hand," I demanded, and she complied. I felt her soft, feminine hand in mine. I squeezed it firmly and said, "Now I have you and I will see if you are real when I wake up." Once again, I tried to wake up.

As I gradually woke up, her hand ... finger after finger ... disappeared from my hand. When I opened my eyes, my arm was bent at the elbow in front of my face and my fingers were squeezed into a fist, but my hands were empty. The young lady was gone. I was sweating and breathing heavily.

Emotionally distraught, I put on my cassock and went to see my spiritual director, Father Špidlík. I described the intensity of my dream and said that I would leave the seminary at once rather than become a disgrace to the priesthood by having an unlawful woman in my priestly life. I asked for his direction.

"This is a serious matter," he explained. "I cannot give you direction. I have to pray and sleep on it first. Come to see me tomorrow and I will tell you whether you should stay or leave."

The next day he had an answer for me. "Stay here. Do not leave. Definitely you have a priestly vocation.

We don't know about the future, but the future will take care of itself." That put me at peace again and I could joyfully continue my lifestyle and my studies toward the priesthood.

On three occasions I had the opportunity to meet Pope Pius XII face to face. On one occasion, our eyes met on a deeper, personal level and I recognized that he was a holy man. There was depth, softness and at the same time, aristocratic superiority in his eyes—a strictness and natural authoritative attitude. Indeed, he was an aristocrat—obviously attached to the external legal structures and inflexible procedures of the Church.

I was ordained to the priesthood at the Lateran Basilica on March 1, 1958, by His Reverence Archbishop Lord Lois Traglia. I was exhausted. The ordination was preceded by a one-week retreat that involved strict fasting in a cold room without sufficient blankets in an unheated Jesuit retreat house. Ordination day was one of the happiest days of my life. In my idealism, I was ready to change the world and bring justice and happiness. I was ready to work in God's vineyard. I completed my studies at the Pontificium Atheneum Lateranense on June 19, 1958, with a diploma and the academic title of Prolyta Cum Laude, which was basically a Masters Degree in Theology that entitled me to teach theology.

23. Bronzolo

YOUNG CZECH AND SLOVAK PRIESTS ORDAINED IN Rome during those communist years could not return home to Czechoslovakia unless they were willing to cooperate with the communists and follow their directions, leading gradually to the destruction of the Church. Their first pastoral assignments were in northern Italy in a mountainous area of Alto Adige, also called Suedtirol, an area of the Alps that until the end of World War I had belonged to Austria.

My first appointment in the summer of 1958 was in the Diocese of Trent in the town of Bronzolo with an Italian and German speaking population. I had the advantage of being neither Italian nor Austrian—an advantage because significant tensions existed between the two groups under the surface.

The Italian parish priest in Bronzolo died before I arrived and his relatives expropriated all his belongings from the old stone rectory. There wasn't even a bed available for me when I arrived. The young assistant priest was Don Vittorino. He welcomed me cordially. In addition to the ordinary tasks of celebrating daily mass, hearing confessions for long hours at the end of each week, and preaching on Sundays, I had to teach religion at the local elementary school, which forced me to improve my Latin. I was paid for the teaching. Otherwise, I had no income except small fees for celebrating masses for the intentions requested by parishioners. The school income allowed me to buy a motorcycle.

The general population of the town was quite poor and unable to support the parish administration; however, there were about six well-to-do Italian and German families on which the parish financially depended. In the past, many of the inhabitants were labourers in a quarry that went out of business. Most of the others were mezzadri, dependent on their contracts with the land owners. A mezzadro worked on the owner's land and shared the crop with him.

I was twenty-nine years old and full of enthusiasm. Finally, after five years in Rome, my hands were free and I could do something more practical for the Kingdom of God than study. I developed a good relationship with the young assistant pastor Don Vittorino. We understood each other well.

He introduced me to the local pastoral activities, including working with local youth. Under the influence of the older generation, the young people of the town were divided into German and Italian groups. Don Vittorino and I discussed how to bring the two together into one large youth group. Both of us agreed that sports activities, soccer in particular, would be the best way.

However, there was neither a soccer field nor a gym ... and there was no money!

Don Vittorino appointed me chaplain of the local ACLI branch. ACLI was an Italian organization of Catholic workers, an ideological opposite to the Italian Communist party workers' union. At that time, the Communist party in Italy was the largest Communist party in Europe. People were attracted to communism's ideal of justice and equality for all people, the general population's practical way out of poverty and misery.

Our ACLI leadership group held monthly meetings in a mortuary of an abandoned church. There were about eight of us on the committee. One of our goals was to provide some kind of sports facility in the town to get young people together. The members of the committee told me that the idea of uniting young people with the help of sports was over twenty years old. Except for talking about it again and again, nothing ever happened. No one knew how it could be done without a lot of money.

Bronzolo was home to an active Communist party group led by young men from poor families. Their superiors and their command centre were in the nearby city of Bolzano. I knew more about communism than they did. To me as a priest, the individual communists were human souls like everybody else. Although I was a staunch enemy of the communists' "scientific" ideology rooted in atheism, I was not an enemy of communists as individuals. Their main reason for being communist was the poverty into which they were born—the silent humiliation of belonging to the lowest class in the socio-economic pyramid without much chance for improvement in a basically capitalist society.

In my cassock, which was my normal dress, I would visit the tavern across the street from the church. After all, quite a few of the Catholic men went there on Sundays while their wives and children attended mass.

I was confronted in the tavern one time because a priest was not wanted there. I was sitting at the bar and facing the bartender who was standing in front of a large mirror. The bartender winked at me. In the mirror I saw an angry man approaching from behind me, obviously planning to attack me. I quickly turned on my seat and confronted him. He stopped. Then he threatened, "We are going to cut your throat!"

"Is that so?" I replied. "Sit down."

Turning to the bartender, I nonchalantly said, "Pour him a drink." The place became silent. Everybody was watching. The man was taken by surprise.

"We communists cut the throats of many priests[7] after the war," he continued, "and we're going to do it again. I have done it. Four of us drove in a Jeep one night to a rectory and that was the end of the priest."

"Why did you do it?"

He scowled. "Because you priests are always on the side of rich, helping them to oppress us poor people."

As we were exchanging views, the man gradually cooled down. "Do not worry, don Giorgio," he finally said. "You are different. It will not happen to you. I will look after you; I will protect you. You are a good priest."

The other guests in the tavern were listening.

"Thank you for wanting to defend me," I replied, "but you won't be able to. If the present political situation in Italy deteriorates so far that the communists take over, your leaders will command you to murder priests again. If you refuse, they will assign you to an area where nobody knows you and where you don't know the priest. Someone like you will be assigned to Bronzolo, and he will cut my throat."

My new friend, a self-confessed murderer who up to now had escaped justice, had never considered such a possibility. Part of his heart was soft and well meaning, but he was angry.

Some of the local young communists started to trust me. They revealed that their party was receiving significant financial support from the Czechoslovak government. For example, the government was supplying them gratis with large amounts of paper for their propaganda in Italy. They spoke about their radio programs broadcasting to Italy from a radio station in Czechoslovakia.

I never broke the trust of the Communist party members in Bronzolo. On several occasions I observed that some of their local leaders' statements presupposed knowledge of what we had discussed behind closed doors at our ACLI meetings. We held our meetings in an old stone mortuary building. I tried to figure out if there were listening devices in the room. It was a sparse room. There was a bulb hanging from the ceiling, a table and chairs. Neither the stone walls nor the simple furniture offered any hiding place for an electronic listening bug. I concluded that one of the committee members must be a communist.

Who could it be? I searched my mind, imagining each member several times. Then it came to me. Is it the secretary? It couldn't be him; he was such a nice, intelligent, church going Catholic. I must be mistaken. It couldn't be! *"Oh yes, it is,"* my mind kept telling me. Now I had a problem. How was I going to proceed with such an uncertain and delicate matter when I was only guessing? *I must be very decisive and unyielding*, my mind told me ... or was it my guardian angel speaking internally to me? I did not know, but I knew I had to act.

I called our ACLI secretary to the rectory for a private meeting. He was polite and pleasant. As we sat opposite each other, I looked him in the eye and asked, "What are you doing?"

"What do you mean?" he said with a surprised look. "I don't know what you're talking about." A painful discussion followed. I pretended that I knew everything, although I feared that I might be mistaken. Finally he broke down and began justifying himself.

He told me that he was from a poor family. As a youngster he wanted to study, which was why he wanted to enter a seminary for young clerics where he could study gratis. But the parish priest had a special relationship with another family. The priest had arranged for entrance into the minor seminary for one of their less capable sons instead of our ACLI secretary. His revenge against the politics of the Church was his secret service for the communists as a member of the ACLI.

I promised my vengeful friend not to say anything to anybody under one condition—that he immediately resign his secretarial position and cancel his ACLI membership. He did so and I have kept my word until now, fifty-four years later. Even now, I am not revealing his name. I cannot ... I have forgotten it.

Not long after the incident with the ACLI secretary, the young president of the local Communist chapter revealed to me that they had received an order from their leaders in Bolzano prohibiting them from having any contact with me. In spite of that order, our contact continued.

24. Soccer Playground

I REGULARLY WENT TO CONFESSION TO AN OLD monk in the Capuchin monastery in Bolzano. Later on, for some practical reasons, I switched my devotional practice to Monsignor Bortolotti, who lived in an apartment in Bolzano. He was also the chaplain of the ACLI. We developed a friendly and mutually trusting relationship. I discussed with him our desire to get the German and Italian young people together. The problem was money. We had none. The Monsignor suggested that the Italian army could possibly help. He advised me that approaching the army by ordinary bureaucratic government channels in Rome would be naive. It would go nowhere.

Bolzano was home to military barracks and also a military chaplain. The Monsignor suggested I had nothing to lose by speaking with him, so I went to see the military chaplain for advice on how to proceed. I told him about our youth problem in Bronzolo. I explained that the rectory owned a piece of useless, upward sloping land full of large stones in the shadow of a mountain. If we could bulldoze half of the slope and fill in the lower part, we could create a flat area large enough for a modest soccer field. In the winter it could be flooded for a skating rink. By doing this work, the Italian army could perform a service to the public.

The chaplain listened carefully. He agreed that a formal request for the army's help sent to the government in Rome through proper channels would go nowhere. "You came here just at the right time," he told me. "NATO is conducting maneuvers in the mountains, and its supreme commander is staying here in Bolzano. If you are not afraid to talk to him, preferably in front of the Italian generals, you might get the help you are seeking. The Italian generals would not embarrass themselves in front of the commander by producing excuses or explanations for not being able to help."

I thanked the chaplain, mounted my motorbike and returned to Bronzolo. I spoke to Don Vittorino, and together we composed a brief letter that he typed and I signed. In the letter we used proper military titles recommended by the chaplain. With the letter in hand, I returned to the Bolzano.

The entrance to the barracks was guarded by a sergeant and two soldiers. I asked for an audience with His Excellency the NATO Commander. Immediately I got the attention and respect from the officer in charge of the entrance. He said that it was impossible to meet His Excellency at the moment because he was in a conference with the Italian generals. However, if the matter was militarily urgent, the sergeant would interrupt the conference and give the commander my letter.

I panicked for a second. Am I being too aggressive and going too far? But I must not back out! I must finish what I started. Putting on a self-assured face, I asked the sergeant not to interrupt the conference, but to deliver my letter to His Excellency immediately after the meeting, while the military staff was still present. He did so.

A few days later, a colonel arrived in Bronzolo to see me. He saluted me, and in my cassock, I responded with the same salute. I hoped he would think that I had some military background. Mutual respect was essential. I showed the colonel the useless parish property. The colonel set up his conditions: We had to provide good food and accommodations for three soldiers who would do the work, and also provide fuel and safe storage for the bulldozer at night.

I accepted his conditions, although I wasn't sure how I would meet them. I knew that my two Italian colleague priests, Don Tamburini, who would soon be our parish priest, and Don Vittorino would support me. The project was no longer mine, but ours. Nevertheless, I remained in charge of it because the soldiers related to me without paying much attention to other clergy.

The ACLI committee members let the parishioners know from the pulpit what was taking place and requested their cooperation. It created a lot of excitement in the town. The farming people promised to provide the diesel fuel and food for the soldiers. We provided accommodations in a dilapidated upstairs room in our old rectory. I tested the old tiled stove. It worked. The weather was freezing during the nights. Eventually three soldiers arrived with their bulldozer. People young and old gathered around them. The town became alive.

The three young Italian soldiers never complained about anything. They were modest with a good sense of humour. Obviously they were glad to be out of their barracks and on their own. And they meant business.

After a week of work, the bulldozer broke down. Everything stopped and the colonel, who was a professional engineer, arrived. He wanted to know why the bulldozer had broken down. The problem wasn't the large boulders, but the ground. The bulldozer could not move the frozen ground that was firm and elastic like rubber. I was informed that the work had to stop until spring. The colonel confessed that he had experience with technically challenging situations, but he had never dealt with frozen ground like this.

I was afraid that if we stopped the work and the soldiers with their bulldozer returned to their barracks we probably wouldn't see them again. The military would make some excuse and the project would be forgotten. A solution had to be found immediately.

If we can make cracks in the frozen ground, I thought, *the bulldozer could handle it.* The question was how to make the cracks. Dynamite was the answer. For years, men in Bronzolo had worked in a nearby quarry. There must be men who know how to work with dynamite.

I was right. Not only did I find them, but they told me where to find dynamite left over from the closed quarry and where to find a blasting expert. I drove there and back on my motorbike with donated sticks of dynamite under my seat. The detonators were provided by the blasting expert.

Now a new problem arose. The quarry men explained that small stones would be flying in the air from the blasts. The future playground was located at the edge of the town and people could be hurt by the stones. I went to see Francesco, the local police commander, with whom I was on friendly terms, and explained the situation.

"Don Giorgio," he said, "what you are asking me to do is illegal. We would need special permission from a higher authority. It would mean bureaucracy and lots of waiting, and we probably wouldn't get permission anyway. Therefore, I accept personal responsibility and I will do my best for you. I will use my men to stand guard while you're blasting. The blasting must be done at the least dangerous time of the day when not many people are around. It must be well co-ordinated and done quickly."

I informed the colonel that we would make cracks in the frozen ground, and then we would see whether the bulldozer work was possible. He accepted my proposal and repaired the bulldozer. The blasting worked well and the bulldozer finished its work before the snow fell. As the men predicted, some small stones landed on the roofs of nearby houses, but no damage was done and no one was hurt.

Another problem arose. The Communist party, which claimed that it worked for the benefit for ordinary people, stepped in. Its local leadership told me they would report and charge the police commander for criminal behaviour for being on the side of the irresponsible priests who seriously endangered the lives of the people. So much for the communists caring about ordinary people. As long as I was in Bronzolo, and that was until September, 1959, no charges were laid. If they were laid, they got lost somewhere in the judicial administration.

The playground project required more money and more work. We had to make its rough surface smooth and plant grass, build a cabin, and erect a fence. That required determination, creative thinking, patience, perseverance, and most of all, money. But it was no longer up to me. I left Bronzolo to join the Jesuits in Austria. Before I left, several soccer games were played on the rough field.

In the late 1970s, my wife Vera and I took a four-week tour of western Europe. The only other time she'd been overseas was when she went to England for the coronation of Queen Elizabeth as a representative of Newfoundland with several other young ladies. In a period of four weeks, we drove in a camper from Holland, through Belgium, France, Switzerland, Austria and Italy.

In France she wanted to see the area where her father, an officer of the Newfoundland Regiment, was seriously wounded and taken into captivity by the German Red Cross during World War I. We visited the Canadian battlefields and military cemeteries.

While returning from Italy, I wanted to see the soccer field in Bronzolo. I was disappointed, but not surprised, to see a vineyard where the soccer playground had been.

25. Popes Pius XII and John XXIII

IN THE SPRING OF 1958, PIUS XII DELIVERED A SUR-
prisingly pessimistic speech about the future of the
Church from the balcony of Santa Maria Maggiore
Basilica in Rome. He did not see light at the end of the
dark tunnel the Church was in. When I left the plaza
that afternoon, I felt anxious, but I shrugged my shoulders, shook off the feelings, and looked optimistically
toward the future. Several months later, I was appointed
assistant pastor in the diocese of Trent in the town
of Bronzolo.

Pius XII stopped appointing new cardinals to his Curia
Romana, because he felt the end of his life was near. He
wanted to leave the future pope the freedom to select his
own men for the various ministries of the Church. Pius
XII died on October 9, 1958.

Nobody was surprised at the death of the exhausted
pontiff, but it did give rise to the question of who would
replace him and how he would handle the difficult situation of the Roman Catholic Church in the modern world.
The lengthy conclave elected seventy-seven-year-old
Angelo Giuseppe Roncalli, the Patriarch of Venice. I was
disappointed. What could we expect from such an old

JIŘÍ (GEORGE) HOŘÁK

man? The cardinals in the conclave obviously did not know how to rectify the stagnant and outdated church, so they chose someone who would not do much and would not live for long. It would provide them with a few years to find a younger, more energetic pope when the old man died. That was how I interpreted the election of this unknown patriarch.

Was I ever mistaken! But not so Monsignor Bortolotti. I used to visit him in Bolzano almost every week. He was enthusiastic when the new pope was elected. "Now," he said, "things will happen in the church ... good things, good changes! I know Angelo Roncalli on a personal basis. Many people will be surprised what this old smiling joker can do." I didn't say anything; I just wondered. I decided to stay where I was posted and carry on with my pastoral activities. However, I began to observe small, positive changes slowly taking place in Rome under the new pope.

In the fall I decided to take some time off to visit Rome. While in Rome, I applied for entry into the Jesuit order. After being interviewed individually by four Jesuits, I was accepted into the novitiate. There was an obstacle, though—the sworn document of my oath promising that I would not enter any religious order for five years after my priestly ordination.

Jurisdiction over me was in the hands of Cardinal Confalonieri. One of his secretaries was Monsignor František Rýpar. We had illegally crossed the Austrian border together with other theology students. He and I knew each other. I contacted him and told him that I had not made a sworn promise not to enter a religious order. As proof, I asked him to pull out my file at the cardinal's office and look at my "sworn" document with a magnifying glass. There he could see the crossed out words that I did not swear. The next day František phoned me and said that the cardinal wanted to see me. The cardinal smiled when we met and gave me his blessing with the words, "Go to the Jesuits."

My accommodations in Rome for the week were at the Collegium Rusicum. Since I had several free days, I asked the Czech Jesuits for money to travel to San Giovanni Rotondo to see what was happening around Padre Pio.

26. Padre Pio

IN 1957 WHILE I WAS STUDYING FOR THE PRIEST-hood in Rome, my friend Josef, who was working in northern Italy, arrived on motorcycle for a visit. He told me about his confession with Padre Pio. I had heard rumours about Padre Pio, but had not taken them seriously. *All the fuss about this monk might be nothing more than some kind of crowd psychosis*, I thought.

Josef told me how he had scrupulously prepared himself for his confession with Padre Pio. When he had finished confessing, Padre Pio asked him if that was all his sins.

"Yes, Padre, that is all," Josef replied.

"No, that is not all," Padre Pio said. He then explained the circumstances of many years earlier when my friend had committed a sin that he had never confessed. Padre Pio asked him if he wanted to include it in his confession. Josef was shocked and shaken.

"Yes, Padre," he said.

Then Padre Pio asked him again if that was all his sins.

"I cannot remember anything else, Padre."

Padre Pio continued, describing the circumstances of another sin. "Do you want to include it in this confession?"

Josef responded, "Yes."

"Now that is all," Padre Pio said. "I absolve you." He then invited Josef for lunch.

I knew Josef, I liked him, and I believed him. After listening to Josef's story, I decided to visit San Giovanni in hopes of meeting Padre Pio face to face.

Padre Pio was internationally known as a charismatic monk, priest, and confessor who could see through people who confessed to him. He was stigmatized, having the five wounds of Christ crucified. Miracles happened with Padre Pio's intercessions. Lay people wanting to go to him for confession needed a ticket and had to wait three months. Catholic clergy had the privilege of waiting only three days.

San Giovanni Rotondo was a small town on the east side of the Italian peninsula. Padre Pio belonged to a small, poor Capuchin monastery. He had his confessional, a simple traditional wooden box at the back of that church.

When I arrived late in the afternoon, the plaza in front of the church was packed with visitors. As a priest, I had no difficulty finding modest accommodations in a private house. Guests in the house were talking with enthusiasm and expectation about Padre Pio. My hosts explained that if I wanted to attend his 6:00 a.m. mass, I would have to arrive an hour early because the church would be packed.

The next morning I saw that my hosts were correct. Padre Pio's mass lasted one hour. I observed him with a critical eye. His behavior was authentic and quietly focused. He wore gloves to cover his bleeding wounds.

Three Franciscan bodyguards accompanied Padre Pio when he walked from the altar at the end of mass. Walking with difficulty because of the pain, he was mobbed by a group of hysterical people trying to rip off pieces of his vestments for souvenirs. This repulsive behaviour kept his bodyguards busy.

It seemed obvious that I had little chance of meeting Padre Pio face to face, not even for a few seconds. When he entered the sacristy, a monk closed the door behind him and stood there to prevent anyone from entering. I approached the monk, explaining that I was a priest visiting for just one day, and that I was interested in Padre Pio's special charismas. I asked if I would be allowed to enter the sacristy to observe him during his thanksgiving prayers after mass.

The guard allowed me in under the condition that I remain standing at the door. What I saw was very simple. Padre Pio sat silently on a chair with his head in his hands, leaning against a table. That was it. I realized that I could expect nothing more. But there was more to come.

One of the bodyguards who saw me in the sacristy found me later in the crowd. "I understand your interest in his way of praying, but you have no appointment with Padre Pio and no opportunity to meet him. Here is a master key to the monastery and to the church. Return the key before you leave town. In thanksgiving after his mass, Padre Pio attends the following mass at the main altar, but in complete privacy. The two upper side wings of the church are closed with glass doors at each end which are locked. He prays there privately in the right wing during the second mass. With this key you can enter the left upper wing and observe him. He won't notice your presence. At the completion of the second mass, he goes for his meal by passing through the choir section in the back of the new church. From there he enters the small upper part of the old church and then goes through a small door to enter the old monastery where his cell is located. You'll have a chance to meet him as he enters the new church."

Armed with the master key, I went to the upper floor of the left wing, opened the glass door, locked it behind me and found a kneeler. In the opposite wing was Padre Pio, motionless, half sitting on a chair, half leaning over the kneeler. His head was bowed; he appeared to be in another world. While the mass downstairs was in progress, he remained motionless except to raise his head when the bread and the wine were consecrated.

When the mass was over, Padre Pio walked through the door to the back of the church. I did the same on the opposite side of the church, hoping to meet him, but there were already a dozen men waiting for him. A few aggressively tried to get his attention, asking questions as he walked by. They were trying to kiss his hand, but he wasn't very cooperative with some of them. He answered some questions, but not others. I observed the scene from the back of this group.

This seemingly lifeless and relaxed monk suddenly became an energetic man with a clear, articulate voice, speaking an Italian dialect. He turned to a young man in a cassock and reprimanded him in a commanding voice. "No! That's not the way to proceed. You are wrong!" The young man burst into tears.

Padre Pio continued through the narrow door into the old monastery. Most of us managed to kiss his gloved hand before he entered. When he opened the door, the group tried to follow him. I managed to be the third one who followed behind him down a narrow corridor.

The first man behind Padre Pio was aggressive. He attempted to kiss Padre Pio's hand, who denied him by swiftly raising his hand above his head. The man then reached for Padre Pio's hand. Padre Pio turned to him angrily.

"What you are doing is wrong," he said. "If you don't believe me, ask the gentleman behind you. He is a lawyer."

The rebuked man froze. Padre Pio took a few steps forward and quietly turned to the shocked man. "If you succeed in your affairs, where will you be in a year?" He then continued his slow walk to the refectory.

I stopped at Padre Pio's cell. It was a small room, about ten by seven feet, with a small window, a table, a chair and a clothes hanger. That was all. How modestly this holy monk lived, a monk to whom money was pouring in from around the world! It was obvious that he was living mentally and emotionally on a higher level of consciousness.

It was noon and the monk community gathered for lunch. I was waiting on the second floor corridor to return the master key to the friendly guard. Out of the window facing the plaza in front of the church I could see local people begging for money.

Standing there contemplating the spectacle, I felt someone join me. It was Padre Pio. He initiated the conversation.

"Look at them. What a shame! There they are, begging instead of working."

I was surprised by his harsh tone; however, I had something else in mind and didn't hesitate to take the opportunity to ask this clairvoyant priest. "Padre Pio, what is the main mission of a Catholic priest?"

He turned to me so that we were eye to eye. I looked into the deep, calm eyes of a man full of energy.

"You, a priest, are asking me such a question?" he replied. "Don't you know? Sanctificare!" He paused a moment and then headed down the corridor.

I stood motionless, pondering my good fortune and his answer. As I understand it, sanctificare means helping people grow to a higher realm of holiness, of consciousness.

I felt an inner peace. Guided by a higher power, I had been granted an encounter with a man of God. I returned the key to the good monk and left for Rome with a grateful heart.

27. Ortler Mountain

WHEN I RETURNED TO NORTHERN ITALY FROM Rome, I reported to the Vicar General of the diocese of Trent. I informed him that I had received permission from the cardinal to join the Jesuit order and that the Jesuits were sending me to their novitiate in Austria. The Vicar General discharged me from my duties in Bronzolo. I remained in Bronzolo for awhile, waiting for directions from the Czech Jesuits in Rome. Meanwhile, I contacted Fr. František Štaud, a Czech priest who had graduated from Nepomucenum and was in charge of the small mountain parish in the village of Trafoi.

Trafoi is located 1540 metres above sea level under the highest Italian alpine peak named Ortler, 3905 metres high. I love mountains. My first climbing experience was in the company of my friend Vilém, in Slovakia in the summer of 1949. On our feet and hands, we reached the summit of Lomnický Štít, over 2600 metres high. In the summer of 1950, we climbed Gerlach, a little bit higher than the Lomnický Štít. Not long after my ordination, I climbed with a young mountain guide to the summit of Eldechce in Sued Tirol. I was determined to climb Ortler.

Father Štaud had an adventurous spirit. He participated in avalanche rescue parties which earned him the respect of the local German speaking population. I phoned to ask if I could spend a few weeks with him before I was called to Rome.

I arrived in Trafoi on my motorcycle. At that time I was practicing certain forms of asceticism such as wearing sharp chains on my stomach and under my knees. Not far from Trafoi on a gravel road, I had to turn right onto a bridge over a deep valley. While making the right turn, the pain was so sharp that I almost lost control of the motorcycle. I barely managed to make the turn. After I crossed the bridge, I stopped. No one was around. I took off the chains and threw them into the abyss, rejecting my dangerous ascetic foolishness.

Father Štaud welcomed me to his old rectory which housed a classroom for the local children. The house was highly disorganized, a real mess, except for the classroom. The dear priest thought this was normal. With his permission and co-operation, I moved furniture, painted, and chiselled the stone walls to install electric plugs and lights. Father Štaud was impressed and highly appreciative when I finished. He thanked me, and as a reward he arranged a trip to the top of Ortler Mountain with a certified, experienced guide. The Italian army officers had to follow his directions when they were maneuvering in the mountains. He spoke to me in German, his native language.

The guide arrived in the morning accompanied by a young woman who was also an experienced climber. He was a bit hesitant about whether we should climb Ortler peak because he saw fresh snow. After all, it was late September already. They decided we would begin the journey and see how far we got. After checking my boots and my clothing, we set out. The climb to the peak took two days, the way back home to Trafoi only one day. On the way up and on the way down, I learned quite a bit about life in the high mountains through the stories they told me. The experience was strenuous, but joyful, beautiful and worthwhile.

We spent a night on the highest mountain lodge in the Italian Alps—no electricity, no firewood, just rocks all around. I was so cold I couldn't sleep. The next day after breakfast we tackled the second stage of our climb. The guide roped me onto a long line that was connected to the woman behind me. With his mountain ax, he chiselled step after step into the glacier. I followed behind him. After hours of rigorous climbing, we reached the peak of Ortler.

What a silent and peaceful joy—the joy of victory without bloodshed. The silence was deep and solid. Our careful descent was joyful. They showed me a small emergency hut built from ice that had saved mountaineers' lives when they were caught by sudden snowstorms. In a sudden freezing storm, visibility would be cut to zero because of the wind and flying snow; the climbers had to spend one or two days in the ice hut, depending on weather conditions. We were fortunate to make it back in good weather without any problems.

We were happy and energized when we returned. As an inexperienced climber, I was especially joyful and grateful to be home safe and sound after conquering the highest peak in the Italian Alps.

V. AUSTRIA AGAIN

28. Goodbye Italy

From trafoi I returned briefly to Bronzolo. I took a speed train from Bronzolo to Rome where I settled for a few days in Collegium Rusicum. I left my motorcycle and my meagre possessions, mostly books, with the Czech Jesuits. I was poor again, but only materially, so I did not mind. I obtained a temporary Italian travel passport, got an Austrian visa and departed on a speed train for Innsbruck, Austria. My spiritual director, Tomáš Špidlík, S.J., accompanied me to the Rome railroad station and waved goodbye.

In Innsbruck, I stopped at the international Jesuit College and visited for a few days with Stanislav Florian who was married to an Austrian woman. He had returned from Venezuela, settled in Innsbruck and opened his own laundry business. I also spent time with Father Vladimír Richter, S.J., a university professor. He was healthy again after recent open heart surgery. Open heart surgery at that time was something new, and was considered very risky. One of the cardiologists who assisted with his operation was a young Austrian doctor who had a private heart clinic in Vienna. He knew Father Richter not only on a professional basis, but also as a friend. I complained to Father Richter about my heart acting up from time to time with pains and an irregular beat. It was a privilege for me to be referred to his physician friend, a highly respected cardiologist in Vienna.

When I arrived in Vienna, I had to wait at the heart clinic for several hours. After tests and X-rays, the cardiologist examined me and wrote a prescription. It was late in the evening when I left the clinic, and I wanted to take a night train to the Austrian Jesuit College and novitiate in St. Andrea. I had no time to search for a pharmacy to get the prescription filled; I thought there would be a pharmacy at the Vienna railroad station. Indeed, there was one, but a sign on the door indicated the pharmacy was closed for the night and gave directions to the nearest open pharmacy. I had no time to search for the nearest pharmacy because my train was about to leave. I decided to get the heart medication in St. Andrea.

In the morning, I arrived at the Jesuit College in St. Andrea and met my novice master, Father Josef Muehler, S.J. He was an ex-soldier from the German army. I told him that I needed the heart medication that was prescribed for me in Vienna. He explained that there was no pharmacy in St. Andrea, but that two medical practitioners in town were taking care of prescriptions. He referred me to Dr. Schweiger, a gentleman about sixty years old.

I gave the doctor my prescription; he looked at it and then looked back at me.

"Who gave you this?" he asked.

I told him it was the doctor in Vienna.

"Yes, I see his name right here. This doctor didn't see you," he replied.

"What do you mean? I had a thorough medical examination by him."

"Yes," said the old doctor, "that doctor saw your heart, but he did not see you. He could teach me about the heart, but not about people. You are completely exhausted. If I fill out this prescription, you will become addicted to it for the rest of your life. If you agree, I will prescribe a different medicine. If my medicine doesn't work, I will fill this prescription for you."

I was surprised, but agreed to his proposition. His prescription consisted of a large bottle of vitamins, a half hour walk in the country air after lunch, and up to two hours of sleep in the afternoon. I presented the new prescription to my novice master and he respected it. In two months I was fine; my heart started to beat regularly and I didn't need the medication prescribed by the doctor in Vienna.

That was the beginning of my Jesuit novitiate.

29. Jesuit Novitiate

THE JESUITS WERE THE LAST ORDER CREATED IN the Roman Catholic Church. An order is characterized by its unique rules of religious lifestyle. The Jesuits were founded in the sixteenth century by Ignatius of Loyola, a Basque aristocrat and soldier, who journeyed deep into his own psyche while recovering at his home castle from a wound suffered during a battle with the French.

After the Jesuits, no other religious orders were created in the Church, but rather religious congregations. There are many congregations that operate with their own rules composed of historically tested religious rules, like Benedictines, Carmelites, Augustinians, Franciscans, Dominicans and Jesuits. All of them, orders and congregations, take vows of poverty, chastity and obedience. Members of an order may be legally considered monks. That doesn't mean that automatically all of them are monks spiritually. Becoming a true monk requires more than belonging to a religious order. A religious path is a good path towards monkhood. I aspired to become a true monk.

The Jesuit novitiate normally lasts two years. In my case it lasted for two and half years. Father Prešeren S.J., assistant to Father General for the Slavic branch of the Jesuits in Rome, forgot about my existence. That was the explanation given to me with apologies when I inquired what was happening. It was an administrative problem. I learned that my next assignment would be in Rhodesia, Africa.

The novitiate consisted of learning about the Jesuit way of life: how to live together in a community joyfully and peacefully, how to be obedient, dependable, and at the same time, how to be independent. It is not easy; the ideal is high. It means practicing various ascetic disciplines like patience, obedience, tolerance of physical and mental pain, humility and endurance.

The most difficult exercise for me was sitting on a chair surrounded by other novices criticizing my shortcomings in my striving for the ideal of spiritual perfection. I had to remain silent without the right to defend myself against their ridiculous accusations and criticisms. I survived it and was accepted into the Jesuit order.

30. Habitus Non Facit Monachum

Habitus non facit monachum.
Dress does not make a monk.

BEFORE RELATING MY EXPERIENCES WITH MONKS, I will share a few related stories.

In ancient China, large non-Christian monasteries were supported by the emperors who valued the monastic formation of good and wise citizens. Some of the ex-monks became the emperors' most reliable, well disciplined civil servants.

An emperor decided to pay a visit to a monastery of more than a thousand monks. At the end of his visit, he congratulated the abbot for his excellent work in educating so many young monks.

"Your Excellency," replied the abbot, "from the thousand here, there will be only three, maybe four, real monks."

Normally, a religious community's discipline is very important in the initial stages of a true monk's formation. *Autobiography of a Yogi* deserves reading and deep reflection. It is available on the Internet. Another small book that deserves attention and reflection, leading to the contemplation of Christ's universal presence, is *The Universal Christ* by Bede Griffiths, a true monk. To absorb and digest this book in meditation is a solid foundation for moving into the depths of Christian spirituality.

To be a real monk is a very special and privileged vocation, not dependent on monastic life only or on the sex of the person. A good nun can become a true monk.

Modern Christianity continues to be in a new developmental stage as it embraces a more ecumenical orientation; it is in the process of cleansing and maturing.

A Jesuit missionary in Japan once told me that several Buddhist monks regularly meditated on the floor in the back of their church. When they were asked why they were coming to a Roman Catholic Church to meditate, they explained that for some unknown reason, the best atmosphere for their meditation existed there. They probably felt that way because the prayers of so many people created a special, pure, spiritual atmosphere—quite the opposite of our noisy environment of advertising, business and money chasing, and running faster and faster as neurotics often do. The central point of the chapel was the Eucharistic presence of Christ in the tabernacle which would only add to the pure, holy atmosphere the monks experienced.

I lived a great part of my life in large cities, mostly for employment reasons, and I had a desire to settle in the country, close to nature. Years later, when I was married,

Vera had no objections to moving out of the city, so we sold our four-bedroom townhouse in Mississauga and built a house on some land on the outskirts of Durham, Ontario, northwest of Toronto. Our property bordered a large provincial conservation area with walking paths, camping facilities, and a river forming a lake with water-falls. In the bush on our property, I built a hermitage. In that hermitage, Vera or I often spent two nights and one day in silence and solitude with no telephone, no radio, and no books except the Bible. A few guests spent time there in solitude as well. This peaceful haven allowed me to continue with the spiritual disciplines of a true monk.

When I was thirteen, I seriously injured my right knee as a goaltender in handball. After surgery, I spent four-teen days in the Children's Hospital in Brno. I had no problem with the knee until one day in the 1980s when I was meeting my family in Yugoslavia. Suddenly, while driving a car, I experienced a sharp pain in that knee, but I didn't see a doctor in Yugoslavia. After I returned to Canada, I had another surgery on that knee at Women's College Hospital in Toronto. An older surgeon there reassured me that I had nothing to worry about because the muscles in my legs were strong and would support the damaged knee cartilage. In his opinion, the next surgery on the knee would not be necessary for another five years.

Seven years later I was in trouble with that knee again. This time I was referred to the General Hospital in

Kitchener, Ontario. They took the necessary X-rays and set up a date for the next surgery. At that time I was regularly driving to a swimming pool at the YMCA in Owen Sound, a larger town north of Durham.

Just before the surgery, it was my weekend to spend the day and two nights in our hermitage. As usual, I had my four thirty-minute silent sitting sessions of meditative icon-contemplation. During one of those sessions, I was surprised by a calm, pleasant presence. I was not alone! Six monks, probably Buddhists, with brown skin and of small stature, silently sat cross legged, three on each side of me.

Hallucination? Perhaps, but my mind was clear and quiet. Without spoken words, they were giving me a silent message: "We will help you. You don't need the surgery. We will help you."

In a reverent manner, I bowed to them and said, "I appreciate your kindness. Thank you! My way is different than yours. I do not want to offend you, but I did not call for you. Leave me in peace as I am leaving you in peace."

When I said this silently and quietly, they disappeared as quickly as they had appeared. Once again ...hallucination? I know about hallucinations under the influence of heavy medication in the hospital. I knew that I was hallucinating, but I couldn't control it. The problem was in my brain.

Two days later, I drove to Owen Sound for my swimming session. As I was leaving the YMCA, I noticed a yellow leaflet on a counter advertising Tai-Ky-Do, an aggressive Japanese form of Tai-Chi martial arts. My reaction was negative—I was not interested. I had experienced enough of these approaches to spirituality and health. After all, our Christian faith has its own mystical traditions focused on Jesus and His mother Mary.

As I was driving home, I was flooded with guilt. The words kept coming to me: "There you are, you arrogant, conceited man. What do you know about what you just rejected? Nothing!" The feelings of guilt grew and grew. Finally, to stop the mental torture, I made a U-turn in the middle of the road and returned to the YMCA. I picked up a copy of the yellow leaflet and drove to Durham. After I read it, I decided to explore Tai-Ky-Do.

The Tai-Ky-Do was taught by John, a Japanese fellow who called himself a sensei. I told him that I could not do his exercises because of my knee and my heart condition. He asked me to sit down and observe. After the session with his adult students, he turned his attention to me and asked about my problem.

I explained my medical problems and the up-coming knee surgery, and he revealed that he was from an old traditional Japanese medical family that had perished in the Nagasaki nuclear disaster. His father was not interested in medicine, but John had learned from his grandfather.

Then he said while demonstrating, "Stand up straight, push your pelvis forward, turn your damaged right foot to the right as far as you can, and start walking slowly, taking small steps. With this exercise, you will transfer the weight of your body to the right cartilage in the knee, and the pain will disappear." I started to practice it immediately.

Two days later I cancelled the knee surgery in Kitchener. That happened twenty-eight years ago. I have not had the knee surgery to this day.

Lucky coincidences! Really? My Japanese teacher claimed to be a married monk, but not a monk in the Christian tradition. I will never forget him. Habitus non facit monachum. Dress does not make a monk. What then makes a formal monk a real monk?

31. Klagenfurt

DURING MY NOVITIATE AS AN ORDAINED PRIEST, I was able to help on Sundays by celebrating mass in the churches in the area of St. Andrea in Lavamthal. My certification from Rome entitling me to hear confessions was not recognized by the Jesuits in Austria. I needed to be re-examined. After all, officially I was only a novice.

The examination took place in a Jesuit community in Klagenfurt, not too far from St. Andrea. It was scheduled for 10:00 a.m. To travel there and back by bus on the same day was no problem. Father Muehler S.J. my novice master, kindly warned me that it was not going to be easy to pass the exam. He said that I need not feel embarrassed if I failed because he had failed twice before succeeding.

In Klagenfurt I received a friendly welcome after which two examiner priests took me to a room. They asked me many questions and presented me with imaginary situations that sometime take place in the confessional. Evidently they had not taken into account that I had spent many hours in confessionals in Italy. The questioning lasted for an hour.

When we finished the examination, they invited me for lunch. It was customary for all the Jesuits of that community to gather at noon in their chapel for a period of silent reflection, followed by the litany of the saints recited loudly. The Klagenfurt community consisted of eight priests and two brothers. They gathered in the chapel, kneeling in prayer.

I was behind them on a kneeler at the back of the chapel with my face in my hands, eyes closed. I felt tired. I was passively listening to the rhythmic answers of the community, "Erbarme Dich unser" (have mercy on us), answering the prayerful invocations of the leader's voice. In my heart I was with them, but I was using neither my voice nor my mind.

In the middle of the prayer, I lifted my head from my hands, opened my eyes and was surprised at what I saw. Over the head of each individual in front of me was a little flame—not a colourful flame, but a colourless, living flame like from vapour or fog, a definite moving, living form. I examined the individual flames. They were similar to each other, but some were larger and more alive than others. Every one of the Jesuits had such a flame over his head. I hoped I had one too, but of course I couldn't see it. The scene reminded me of the tongues of fire over the heads of the apostles in Acts 2:3 in the New Testament.

One of the priests caught my attention. He had only one arm, the right one. The left arm from his shoulder to his fingers was made from dark rubber. He manipulated his rubber arm with his good hand. I wondered how he managed to be ordained a priest with such a handicap.

After lunch, as I was walking and chatting with him alone in the yard, he told me his story. As a Jesuit scholastic after the 1937 Nazi occupation of Austria, he was conscripted into the Wehrmacht, the German army. He was on the front line in September, 1939, when Germany attacked Poland. It was his task to cut the barbed wire on the border. As he lay on his back cutting the wires, he suddenly saw a huge light and was paralyzed. Conscious and without pain, he wondered what had happened.

When the German Red Cross soldiers were putting him on a stretcher, one of them remarked, "The war is over for you, boy." And it was. A Polish bullet had cut off his whole arm except for the main artery on which the arm was hanging. For him, the war lasted only half an hour. As an invalid, he was able to continue his studies in theology and eventually be ordained a priest.

When I returned to the novitiate house in St. Andrea in the afternoon, I reported to my novice master that I had passed the exam and was qualified to hear confessions in Austria. He congratulated me. I didn't mention anything about seeing the flaming tongues over the heads of the Jesuits in the chapel. I was afraid that it would lead to suspicions that I was unstable and unfit to become a Jesuit.

32. St. Ulrich

St. ULRICH IS IN THE SOUTH EASTERN CORNER OF
Austria. It is a town with a Roman Catholic parish in
charge of two other nearby filial churches without a
priest. In my time there, the parish priest of St. Ulrich
was a Jesuit, Father Hassler.

He was an intellectual by nature, an impractical
man destined to be a professor. Unfortunately, Father
Hassler suffered a nervous breakdown. The bishop of the
Klagenfurt area appreciated any help he could get from
the religious clergy. Father Hassler, with the consent of
his superiors, accepted the responsibility for St. Ulrich
parish. It was not far from the large Jesuit community
in St. Andrea. From there he could get help from a priest
whenever necessary.

Father Hassler was a holy man with a great heart for
people and a great commitment to the Church. In his
pastoral dedication, he suffered occasionally from physical exhaustion. People would find him sitting on the side
of a road resting, even in the winter. He had neither car
nor motorcycle; he walked everywhere, unless somebody
gave him a lift. In spite of his good will and caring, he
experienced difficulties with quite a few parishioners who
seldom came to church. His memory was phenomenal,

but keeping well organized written records and files seemed to be too difficult for him.

Some of the windows in his church were broken. Bats loved flying into the building, and sometimes left their droppings on the altar. The rectory, not far from the church, had a leaky roof. It was not heated, except for his bedroom and the small kitchen. It was orderly and clean, thanks to the capable hands of the old Frau Sofie. His office was a large meeting room with a big table in the middle. On that table were piles of papers, important documents, church bulletins, bits of paper with notes and names, old socks, underwear, sausages and dry bread. Only Father Hassler knew where to find what he needed.

Around the church, the cemetery in his charge had graves right at the side entrance of the church door, so that parishioners had to step carefully around or over the graves to get into the church.

On Sundays, I rode a motorbike to the St. Ulrich parish to help out. I celebrated Holy Mass and gave a sermon either in the parish church or in one of the two associated churches. In spite of the administrative confusion, I had a genuine respect for Father Hassler. I liked him for his sincerity, generosity and good will, but sometimes I felt annoyed. He was not crazy ... he had dignity. I understood his psychological disposition and we got along well.

The bishop of the diocese was glad to have a priest for one of his parishes, but he wasn't enthusiastic about Father Hassler's performance. He knew the situation, but he couldn't do much about it. I reported the administrative shortcomings to my superiors in St. Andrea with a proposal: Under obedience, send Father Hassler for a month's vacation, give me three novices as helpers, and I would get the administration of the parish in order. After a few days, I received a reply from my novice master: "Go ahead."

I share this story as one of the pastoral experiences that impacted me. I won't elaborate on what the three novices and I did or how we did it, except to say that the parishioners were co-operative. The windows were fixed, the bats driven out, and a new main entrance and side door installed. The cemetery was mapped out so that not only Father Hassler, but everyone could find where people were buried. The clock on the church tower was working again.

People contributed money generously so that the debt left behind was small and easy to handle. When Father Hassler returned, he did not appreciate the changes. It was humiliating for him. I felt sorry for the humiliation that I had caused, but what else could be done under the circumstances? I thought that I had provided a good service.

One of the medical practitioners who serviced the St. Ulrich and St. Andrea areas was Dr. Schweiger, a country doctor, and the one who placed me on the vitamin diet when I arrived at St. Andrea. He would see sick people at any time, night calls included.

One dark night we met unexpectedly on a lonely, winding, country road—he in his Volkswagen and I on my motorcycle. I stopped by the side of the road and turned off the bike reflector. I needed to empty my bladder. The road was deserted except for an approaching car, whose distant lights snaked up the road. The car stopped and the driver asked me if I needed help. It was Dr. Schweiger returning home from visiting a patient. In the darkness we recognized each other immediately.

The doctor often attended Sunday masses in St. Andrea, and other times in St. Ulrich at its filial churches. I was told by some local people that as a young medical practitioner, he used to be quite wild and arrogant. After his first marriage failed, he remarried and experienced a religious conversion. His attitude changed completely, perhaps under the influence of his new wife who understood him well.

One Sunday, the doctor offered to drive me to one of the filial churches. I was waiting for him in front of his house when his ten-year-old son dashed out of the house right into the middle of the road without looking left or right.

"How many times have I told you that you must look first left and right?" his father shouted. "I will help you to remember." He put the boy on his knee right there in front of his mother and me and gave him a spanking on his behind. Then he ordered him into the car without paying any attention to his tears. I approved. Dr. Spock would not approve ... or would he? I read somewhere that he treated his own children just as my Austrian friend did, not in the way that he preached in his lectures.

On another occasion my doctor friend called me late in the evening. "Near the village of St. Ulrich, an old farmer is dying. Go and see him at once. This is the reason I'm asking you to do this," he said. "Years ago, a tax collector with his briefcase of collected money was returning home on foot. He was tired, so he asked a farmer with horses and a cart if he could ride with him. The farmer agreed and the tax collector fell asleep. While he slept, his briefcase disappeared. It probably fell on the road. Another farmer, this dying old man, was following at a distance with his horses on the same road. He probably found the briefcase. Nothing could be proven, but not long after, the second farmer started to buy more fields. The tax collector's wages were garnished for the rest of his employment. Don't tell anybody that I told you this story, but go there at once because by morning the farmer might be dead."

So off into the night I went. When I opened the door of the farmhouse, a boy in a panic shouted, "Der Pharrer ist hier!" I introduced myself and said that I wanted to see the sick man. The lady of the house didn't know what to do as I was not expected. With some hesitation, she took me to a room with only one light bulb hanging from the ceiling where the man was lying in bed.

He was surprised, but not hostile. We started to talk. I asked his wife to leave the room and she reluctantly did. We talked and talked. The old man was excited, glad to see me, red faced, but friendly. Finally, after about two hours, I left.

Doctor Schweiger phoned me the next morning wanting to know what had happened. When I described the scene and explained that I had spent two hours with the patient, he called me irresponsible because the man could have died at any moment. He had sent me to the farm for a brief visit, probably to administer the sacrament of the dying. The old farmer's extended family was already gathering for his funeral.

A few days later, the old man arrived at morning mass with a cane, a big smile on his face. I also was smiling and wondering what had happened. I did not know. There was no funeral.

On some Sundays I had to celebrate two masses, one in the village of St. Ulrich and then another mass in an affiliated church. At that time, before Vatican II, a priest and all the faithful were obliged to fast from food and drink from midnight until Holy Communion the next day. After Holy Communion, the faithful were expected to continue abstaining from food and drink for another fifteen minutes. The same rule applied to priests.

Very few people came to Holy Communion, often because they had not gone to confession first. Maybe one or two, occasionally three individuals came for communion in the St. Ulrich parish. Another liturgical rule prohibited keeping the Eucharist in any church where there was not at least one person visiting for a brief adoration prayer every day. As well, the red light had to be burning in front of the tabernacle.

One Sunday, my second mass at the filial church was scheduled for two hours after my first one. I was hungry, thirsty and tired. While dressing in the sacristy, I usually put three small hosts on the patena (the small golden plate on the top of the chalice), because it was easy to consume them in case nobody came to Holy Communion. On this particular Sunday in the sacristy before the mass, twelve little hosts slipped from my hand onto the patena instead of three. In my tired mood, I just let it be with the thought that I would handle it somehow, even if nobody came to communion.

The mass was said in Latin with the priest's back toward the people. When communion time came, I turned toward the people with the words, "Ecce Agnus Dei, ecce qui tollit pecata mundi" (This is the Lamb of God who takes away the sins of the world). Nobody came forward for communion.

I turned back toward the altar thinking, *You stupid man, you should have foreseen that this might happen. Now what will you do with the twelve hosts and your dry mouth? That's too many. Well, get at it and consume them yourself!*

I bent down to the altar to put three consecrated hosts in my mouth. As I was lifting them towards my mouth, I heard a commanding voice coming from inside saying, "No!" I stopped. I was surprised and became alert. I started again by bending down over the altar to put the three consecrated hosts in my mouth, and again the same commanding voice said, "No!" *Am I going crazy? I wondered. Am I sick? Hallucinating? What's happening to me? I must overcome this whatever the cost.*

I tried for the third time to consume the consecrated hosts, and the same thing happened. I panicked for a few seconds, and then I started an inner dialogue with that voice.

"What am I supposed to do? I asked.

"Put the hosts into the tabernacle," the quiet voice answered.

"It is against liturgical rules," I replied. "The church is locked during the week. Nobody comes here. There is no little red lamp hanging from the ceiling. I cannot do it."

"Red light, no red light. Light a candle instead," the voice replied.

I didn't know what else to do but to follow the instruction. I sent one of the altar boys to the sacristy for the tabernacle key. I put the Blessed Sacrament into the tabernacle and lit a candle. I finished the mass facing the people with the blessing, "Ite, missa est" (Go, the mass is ended). Then with the altar boys leading the way, I walked toward the sacristy. An inner torment exploded in my mind. *What is going on here? I have to talk to my novice master about this. He will send me to a psychiatrist and possibly kick me out of the novitiate.*

As I was taking off my vestments in the sacristy and the altar boys were covering the altar with a cloth, a young nun came to the sacristy.

"Father," she said, "we want to receive Holy Communion."

"What? Don't you know that the Blessed Sacrament is not being kept in this church? Where were you when I was offering Holy Communion to the people?"

"We were not here; we came at the end of mass," she replied. "We aren't from here. We are city people on a Sunday picnic. We couldn't find a church and when we did, it was too late."

I teased her a bit. "Gut. This Sunday is an exception. I have Holy Communion for you. Line up at the communion railing."

When I came back to the altar with the tabernacle key, there were eleven teenage girls kneeling at the railing. I was puzzled about what had really happened, but I was happy and grateful. New energy surged in me. A message sounded in my heart: "You see, every one of these little girls is important to Me."

I didn't mention this occurrence to my novice master because I no longer felt that I was going crazy. It was obvious to me that a higher level of Living Reality was at play here, using me and at the same time giving me an important message: "I am with you; do not fear!"

It was one of my happiest days. Jubilant in my heart, I mounted my motorcycle and returned to the Jesuit College in St. Andrea.

VI. CANADA MY DESTINY

33. Austria to Canada

DURING MY NOVITIATE IN AUSTRIA, I DIDN'T KNOW much about the Czech Jesuits in foreign countries. In Czechoslovakia, they were incarcerated, Father Šilhan, their provincial included. But how many of them were outside of Czechoslovakia and where were they? I did not know, except for a few individuals in Rome.

One day in the spring of 1962, I received a letter from Father Feřt S.J., the superior of the Czech Jesuits outside Czechoslovakia, telling me that he was opening a Czech Mission House in Montreal. He asked me whether I would be willing to become a member of his community rather than serving in Rhodesia. My answer was yes.

I crossed the Atlantic from Amsterdam on a noisy Electra four engine propeller plane that carried about sixty passengers. In the back of the plane, which hummed with noisy vibrations, a small group of Jewish people fervently prayed for safety. We were protected. The Electras had a reputation for losing one or two engines during a flight. After a twelve-hour flight, we landed safely at Montreal's Dorval Airport April 16, 1962.

Father Janíček, S.J., a man of few words, was waiting for me. He drove me to the new Czech Mission House built on the grounds of Loyola College, now Concordia University. The college was managed by the Canadian Province of English speaking Jesuits with their provincial residing in Toronto. Along the road from the airport were patches of snow, while in Austria, where I had begun my journey, beautiful wild flowers bloomed.

Canada became my destiny, a better destiny than I could have imagined. Little did I know how my life would change and how different my priestly ministry would be.

The Montreal community of Czech Jesuits existed more in theory than in reality, in spite of the strong efforts of its superior Father Feřt. Its members had been living independently for too many years in different parts of the world.

Father Dostál, a generous intellectual idealist, wanted to become a missionary in China before World War II. To be a Jesuit missionary in China, a Jesuit priest had to spend a preparation period in the French speaking Canadian Jesuit Province. Father Dostál arrived in Canada in 1937, at a time when China was at war with Japan and Mao Tse Tung was promoting his communist regime. Because of those political circumstances, Father Dostál remained in Canada and became a missionary among the Czech immigrants living in North America. He travelled frequently across Canada and often south to the United States. The demand for him was greater than he could manage. Returning home to Czechoslovakia became impossible for him because from 1938 until 1945, Czechoslovakia did not exist as a country, and in September of 1939, World War II started.

Father Janíček belonged to a group of Jesuit students sent in 1946 to Holland in the tradition of the Jesuit's educational system to gain experience in a foreign country. After 1948, this group of Czech and Slovak students could not return home to the communist controlled Czechoslovakia.

After his ordination, Father Janíček landed in Montreal where he was expected to teach mathematics at Loyola High School. It was the early 1950s, and many Czech and Slovak political refugees were arriving in Canada, mostly in Montreal. Father Janíček became their pastor instead of teaching mathematics.

The main focus of his pastoral activities was directed at parents with young children. In co-operation with some of his newly arrived parishioners, he created the Hostýn children's camp in the Laurentian Mountains, about seventy kilometres north of Montreal. Lake Duffy was within walking distance of the camp. That camp is still in operation, although Father Janíček died in 2003. Without his pragmatism, carpentry skills, tools, muscles, and hard work and perseverance, the camp would not have existed.

During the first years of the camp's existence, from the beginning of July almost to the end of August, an average of fifty children slept in the tents. Some mornings in August, the ground and the tents were white with frost. The payment expected from the parents for the children was minimal, in some cases nothing. Parents who could not pay the fee would help around the camp.

My first assignment in Montreal was to learn English and to help Father Janíček with his activities. Camp Hostýn had two areas, one for boys between the ages of six and fourteen, and one for girls of the same age. With hammer and nails, together with Father Kovanda S.J. who was visiting from Rhodesia, and under the supervision of Father Janíček, we built the first and second camp cabins. When the camp opened in July of 1962, I was put in charge of the boys, and Maruška Šmelhausová from Chicago looked after the girls. Maruška and I both had scouting experience in Czechoslovakia which was beneficial. Except for a few scratches here and there, no serious accidents happened in the camp.

At the end of every week, we had a big campfire. Children would entertain themselves and the visiting guests with songs and skits prepared by Father Janíček. He loved this activity and so did the children. Many guests visited from as far away as Chicago, Cleveland, New York, and of course, the Montreal area.

In September I was sent to Regis College in Willowdale, a suburb of Toronto, for two more years of philosophy and theology as a part of my Jesuit formation.

34. Regis College and Texas

THE COMMUNITY OF SCHOLASTICS AT REGIS College consisted of about seventy young men, most of them Americans. Others were English and French speaking Canadians, Europeans from Hungary, Spain, and Belgium, a few Mexicans, and students from India. Since I was already a priest, I was given considerable freedom and flexibility in attending lectures. I also went on temporary assignments anywhere in North America as the need arose.

In spiritual matters, Father David Asselin, S.J., a Quebecois at Regis College, was a great help to me. The young Canadians at the college impressed me as serious and at the same time shy, deferring to the Americans.

During my two years at Regis College, I spent a few weeks in Nakina, a railroad town north of Lake Superior where fish and mosquitoes were the dominant species and snow in June was not uncommon. Then I spent a few weeks in Chicago. During my first night at the parish rectory, there was a shootout on the street outside my window. Two men were killed. At the breakfast table the next morning, the priest explained that it was the Mafia at work. When I asked him how he knew, he said that when the Mafiosi killed someone, they emptied his pockets and pulled them out to let people know who did the killing.

Several times I was sent to Cleveland and once to New York City to fill in for a pastor for three weeks. Most of my time away from the college was spent in Ennis, Texas, a town south of Dallas. These assignments were part of my Jesuit formation in adjustment and flexibility.

I liked Texas. The descendants of the old Czech settlers lived on farms in the area and spoke a Czech dialect. Even some black people could speak Czech. I had several interesting experiences in Texas.

One afternoon I was called to the local hospital because they were having a problem with a Roman Catholic middle class woman in her thirties who had been brutally raped. She was so upset, angry, humiliated and withdrawn that nobody could communicate with her, not even her husband. I sat down quietly beside her bed in a prayerful spirit. In silence, I gently took her hand. After a while, she opened her eyes and looked at me. Her eyes asked whether she was still acceptable after all that had happened. With my eyes and hand contact, without words, I said a respectful "yes." After that she opened up.

She lived in the country in a cluster of three or four houses. Her husband was at work so she was home alone. A man broke into her house, attacked her, tied her to the bed, and raped her several times. She was defenceless. He left her tied to the bed, took her car keys, but was unable to start her car. He returned to the bedroom, untied her, put her in the driver's seat and ordered her to drive.

Once behind the wheel, she had only one obsessive thought: Kill him—even if it cost her own life. She decided to collide head on with the first car they met, but her car wouldn't start. Meanwhile, the neighbours observed that something unusual was happening in her house and called the police and her husband. Her husband and the sheriff tracked the escaped criminal and subdued him.

The medical staff had taken good care of the woman, but they had possibly aborted the beginning of a new life. I agreed with the pragmatic medical staff who took care of the woman that under the circumstances it wasn't appropriate to ask speculative moral questions. I do not support abortion; however, for those who must deal with enigmatic medical problems on the pragmatic level, I ask for understanding and mercy rather than speculative judgments and condemnation.

35. Václav Mareš

To this day, i'm not sure Václav Mareš was the true name of the young man who was introduced to me by Father Botík, the pastor of the Roman Catholic parish of Ennis, Texas.

Václav came to Ennis from the Pentagon in Washington. He was six feet tall, blond, and quite handsome. His English was very limited, almost non-existent. He seemed to be rather introverted, suspicious and taciturn, so it wasn't easy to carry on a conversation with him. It took some time before he told me his story ... a story that contains a precious element—a human heart thirsting for truth, willing to pay whatever cost.

Václav's parents and his extended family were communists, convinced of the righteousness of their cause. He was eighteen when the Communist party, aided by Moscow, took over Czechoslovakia. Václav was accepted into a privileged Marxist-Leninist program for dedicated young communists. His enthusiasm and loyalty led him into a special military program that promised him a rewarding career. He was trained not only in the Marxist-Leninist ideology, but also in operating different kinds of weapons, parachuting and military leadership. He became an officer, and not long after, a high ranking special officer. His zeal for communism as the saviour of the world was authentic. As a trustworthy officer, he was put in command of the border guards. He controlled the electricity of the wire fences around the Czechoslovak borders. Day and night, whenever he was on duty, he kept checking on his subordinate staff. He enjoyed the power and respect due to him as a soldier, as well as his high income and the privileges connected with his position.

Václav started to have serious problems when he was checking on his armed subordinates at nights along the border. He was always accompanied by another officer assigned to him by a higher authority *Why is it that every night a new officer is assigned to me as a companion, an officer whom I do not know and who does not know me?* he wondered. *Why are we so carefully guarding this border? Why are people trying to run away to the corrupted, miserable West? People from the West should be coming to us because we have it so good here. We should open the borders for them so they can run from the West to us.*

These spontaneous questions, born from his privileged position and ignorance of the truth, kept torturing his Marxist-Leninist-ideologically-formed mind. He didn't dare ask for answers and explanations, nor did he mention his thoughts to anybody. These questions eventually became intolerable, so Václav decided to find the answers himself. He didn't see any other way but to cross the border to the West and see with his own eyes what was going on there. He realized that the assignment of another officer as his companion during his duties was nothing but distrust and manipulation by his superiors. He was being watched by the other officer and the officer believed that Václav was watching him. He started to feel that it was an insult to him, a committed communist.

One night he decided to act. He shut off the electricity to the fences without the knowledge of his companion. As they walked along the border, he allowed the other officer to walk a few steps ahead, and then he placed his gun in the officer's back, disarmed him, and ordered him to follow his directions. He was resolved that if the officer resisted, he would shoot him.

Once they were on the Austrian side, they walked to the nearest police outpost. The Austrians recognized their uniforms, realized the situation, and drove them to the Vienna intelligence headquarters. The Czechoslovak government learned almost immediately what had happened and requested the return of both men. The Americans sent the companion officer back to Czechoslovakia and flew Václav to the Pentagon. They knew that if they let him stay in Vienna, he would be found and eventually kidnapped or murdered by the communists.

About twenty years later, I visited Monsignor Botík at his parish in Dallas. I received a warm welcome and great hospitality. In our exchange of experiences and opinions, I asked about Václav. Monsignor Botík explained that Václav had joined the American army and was sent to Vietnam as a paratrooper. After he completed his first term, he applied for a second. After the second one, he applied for a third term. It was granted to him with some reluctance, but nevertheless granted on the basis of his good military record. He had fathered a son in the US during one of his leaves from Vietnam. When his third term in Vietnam was completed, he returned to the US, kidnapped his son, and disappeared somewhere in Europe. His whereabouts were unknown to the monsignor.

Saul, a dedicated Pharisee and an enemy of Christ, became Christ's greatest apostle, yet remained a proud Jew. Pope John XXIII, labelled a modernist by my Dogma professor in Rome, brought life back to the rigid structures of the Roman Church. He created new energy and new life, much to the horror of the super-conservatives. Gorbachev, a thinking communist, may be held responsible for dissolving the decadent idealistic Soviet communist system. Václav, a dedicated and privileged communist, by his thirst for truth became an enemy of the communist system of strict control. Throughout human history, there have always been people like this, which means that our current church situation is not hopeless, and neither is the plight of the human race. Propaganda and brainwashing are effective for controlling masses of ignorant, non-believing people, in spite of their formal education, but there are always individuals from unexpected places prepared to pay a high price for truth and justice. Money is of no value to them, although they need it too. There is no need for pessimism in today's dark world of confusion and uncertainty.

36. Community Problems

NOT LONG AFTER I ARRIVED AT THE JESUIT CZECH Mission House in Montreal in April, 1962, I sensed that something was lacking in our community spirit. Our members were all older men. I was at least ten years younger than the youngest member. I became aware of their complicated and unusual religious lifestyle, mostly because of the political and economic circumstances in the world.

Father Feřt, S.J., the superior of the Mission House, was a devout man who spent his life in structured, well functioning religious institutions, shielded from the roughness of ordinary, worldly life. His main task was to provide spiritual guidance to young people, seminarians and novices. He was an old fashioned idealist; I was a young idealist. He and I understood each other and accepted the benign eccentricities of the individual members of our new community who in their past religious lives were exposed more to individualistic existence than to a community lifestyle. Father Feřt and I believed that it was only a matter of time until a well functioning Jesuit family evolved. After all, each of us in our early years had the same training and knew how Jesuits were supposed to live together.

Unfortunately, it did not work out that way. We looked different as a Jesuit community from the outside than we were in reality. There were no fights among us; however, everyone continued to live in his own personal style. It became impossible to harmonize our group into a cohesive pastoral team.

Each of us can be characterized by a personality type, especially in our later life stages. Imagine a community consisting of an elephant, a fox, a rabbit, an eagle, a chicken, a tiger and a monkey—all of them experiencing the same religious formation in their young idealistic years, and all receiving a cassock and a Roman collar as an outward sign of their goodness, reliability, loyalty and identity. Externally all of them look alike, but internally under the Roman collar, a fox remains a fox, and a monkey remains a monkey. The problems start when a monkey doesn't realize that he is still a monkey, or an elephant forgets that he remains, in spite of his cultivation, an elephant.

This comparison is gross and rough, but clear. The reality of the psychological character differences is fine and subtle. Nothing as drastic as the image I have used existed in our Montreal community, but something similar did exist. There was no malice, but there were serious obstacles.

A superior of a community, if it is a real community rather than a group, has basically two options. One is to command his subordinates as one would soldiers in an army, provoking resistance in the stronger characters and unhealthy submission in the weaker ones. The other option is to harmonize the members under his authority. Practically it means to be their father and mother, and at the same their supervisor and their commander. Very few people appointed as superiors can accomplish that. For that role, they have to be talented, loving saints.

As time went on, Father Feřt became more and more unhappy as he witnessed his dream of a Czech Jesuit community under one roof collapse. He felt helpless. After several years, it all culminated when he locked himself in his room. For several days, nobody knew nor seemed to be interested in what was happening to him.

I decided to go to Toronto to meet Father McDougall, S.J., the provincial of the English speaking Canadian Jesuit Province in the territory where we were located. I explained our situation to him, particularly the emotional condition of Father Feřt. I suggested that Father Feřt be ordered under obedience to return to Radio Vaticana in Rome as soon as possible, because that was where he was happy.

The order came from Rome within a week to the great emotional relief of Father Feřt. He didn't know what I had done nor did he depart at once. He started to breathe normally again, looking forward to his return to Rome. On his recommendation, Father Kovanda S.J., who had returned from Africa, was appointed our new superior.

Unfortunately, Father Feřt never told anybody that the ever-smiling Father Kovanda had suffered two nervous breakdowns and was incapable of handling any emotional pressure. He could celebrate Holy Mass, visit the sick, and hear confessions, but administration was beyond his capability.

Personally, I started to have a problem. I felt uncomfortable and almost guilty for not contributing financially to our house, except the $5.00 for my daily mass intentions. The financial state of our house was unknown to me. It was entirely in the hands of Father Janíček, although the responsibility for it should have been in the hands of the superior, Father Kovanda.

In Ennis, Texas, Father Botík asked again for a priest to help in his parish. He offered financial compensation for this assistance. Since I had already helped out in this parish, I went to Texas. After I settled in the rectory, I realized that what I was doing could be easily done by Father Kovanda, who was very passive. With the consent of Father Botík, I invited Father Kovanda to Ennis and he gladly came. The hot Texas climate suited him.

Now there were two of us. Father Botík offered us an old abandoned rectory in which he expected us to settle permanently. The Texas Jesuit provincial in Fort Worth welcomed us with open arms. Father Kovanda had no objections, but I had two concerns in accepting a permanent settlement in Texas. One was my loyalty to the Mission House in Montreal and the other was the gradual realization of how difficult it would be to get along with Father Kovanda and his misleading permanent smile which concealed his repressed frustration and anger.

Meanwhile, Father Botík welcomed into his rectory another old, lost Polish priest. I was no longer needed, so I gladly returned to Montreal. There I accepted a one-year religion teaching position at the prestigious Loyola High School. It guaranteed a modest but regular income for our house. Another reason I wanted to be in Montreal was because preparations for EXPO 67 were in full swing. Our Mission House could be used for emergency accommodations for visitors coming to EXPO. It would provide us with a bit of extra income.

37. EXPO 67

DURING THE 1966–1967 SCHOOL YEAR, I TAUGHT religion to fifteen and sixteen-year-old students. I wanted them to think on their own and many of them obliged. Of course, that was quite a challenge for me. It was a steep learning curve. It wasn't easy for me to deal with the constant questioning of intelligent youngsters. It would have been much easier teaching mathematics or physics or any other subject, unless I resorted to thoughtless memorization. They were wearing me down. I didn't return to teaching religion at Loyola High School the following year. In order to have more flexibility and bring money into our house, I accepted the student counsellor position at St. Mary's High School. It was much easier than teaching religion.

EXPO was approaching, and our house had to be ready for visitors. With the help of Father Janíček, I set up seven beds for modest overnight emergency accommodation. We expected our future guests to be at the EXPO grounds or somewhere else in Montreal during the day. We would charge $ 2.00 per night, breakfast included. Most of our overnight guests were generous.

The gates of EXPO 67 opened in early spring. It was a great international success, and our plan to have overnight beds available for visitors worked out well. People were coming and going, particularly after the school year was over. One summer evening I received a phone call from Loyola College asking if we had a bed for a young woman, Petronila, visiting EXPO from western Canada. The Jesuits at the college knew her well but had no room to accommodate her. They described her as a respectable person. "Yes, we can accommodate her," I said.

In about ten minutes the doorbell rang and there she was, somehow familiar to me, yet I was meeting her for the first time. Later in the evening I observed her making a long distance phone call. I was impressed with her natural manner and experienced a strong attraction to her. She struck me as a smart, self-confident woman, yet very sad under her friendly, outgoing manner. She asked me to guess her age. She expected me to say something like twenty-two; I said twenty-nine.

"What!" she exclaimed. "Yes, I'm twenty-nine." I realized that I was emotionally in trouble—I was falling in love. She sensed it and responded positively with a friendly smile of understanding. That ignited a storm of conflicting emotions in my heart that I repeatedly tried to calm and control through willpower, reasoning, and strength from my past ascetic practices. This emotional attraction between a religious priest and a woman was totally unacceptable. Now what? How was I going to gently and respectfully get rid of this woman?

The next day under the pretense of being a good host, I accompanied her to the EXPO grounds. I felt quite happy in her company, but that wasn't good. It had to stop! I tried to tell her with sincerity that I was a celibate priest. Little did I know that she had a B.A. in theology and knew a great deal about the Roman Catholic clergy. She listened to my naive explanations patiently and with understanding, acceptance and a smile. That made her even more attractive, creating a deeper conflict in me. In her presence I felt happy.

The following evening, I borrowed Father Dostál's car and took her for a ride. I explained my religious lifestyle, the rules and regulations of religious life and the vow of celibacy. She half listened, smiled and kept chatting. She worked as a psychometrist in a large psychiatric hospital, so she was familiar with the troubles and nervous breakdowns priests and brothers could experience; in spite of this she pretended she didn't understand what I was talking about. She knew better than I did, yet here I was trying to be her teacher.

Our roles eventually reversed. Gently, with friendly smiles and understanding, she started to teach me. I became a baby and a student. She told me repeatedly that she was going to take me down from my soap box. I realized that all my explanations and intellectualizing were not decreasing, but increasing my loving emotions toward her. My head was full of her. I felt that somehow she started to care about me too. *This must stop!* I scolded myself decisively, but it didn't stop. She told me she was expected back in the hospital from her vacation on Monday. I was glad and sorry at the same time. The fire and craziness raged on in my heart.

My suppressed erotic instincts were surfacing. If I gave in to my feelings, there would be far reaching consequences for my religious life and the personal integrity and self-respect that were precious to me. My strong emotions towards her were unacceptable, yet I couldn't liberate myself of them. I decided to run away from her. I didn't know what else to do.

Under the pretense that I had to take some mattresses to Father Janíček's Hostýn camp, I borrowed Father Dostál's car again and said goodbye to her. She came out to help me tie a few mattresses on the roof of the car. We worked together on the task. I liked that too.

I decided to return to Montreal on the Tuesday when she would be gone. To make certain that she was gone, I stayed alone at the camp and returned on Wednesday. When I returned, there she was at our Mission House, waiting for me. She confronted me, frankly stating that she knew my trick and that running away to the camp was contrived to escape the situation. She was right, but not helpful.

Over the next few months we corresponded. I was emotionally trapped, attached to her in spite of her living far away. My religious vows of obedience, poverty and chastity versus her love became a source of ongoing inner torture. If I hadn't been a priest and a Jesuit, this probably would never have happened.

The story continued. I was stubborn and perhaps cruel and rude, insisting that she get married. Her reply was that she would never get married. She'd had several good offers of marriage, but refused them all. I didn't relent. She must get married! Yet another part of me was resisting that idea. My heart was torn and bleeding. *Her marriage will be a solution for me*, I thought. I prayed and asked for liberation from this sweet hell of which I was reluctant to let go. My will prevailed. She must marry to solve my problem.

I realized more than ever how strong a woman can be, and at the same time how vulnerable she becomes. My previous training in self-control was beneficial, yet at the same time inadequate because it was quite self-centred— a form of subtle selfishness in the name of becoming holy. My humility was artificial and unreal. I felt crushed. To practice asceticism is a desirable and commendable thing, but it needs guidance and gentleness, not mere voluntarism

38. Madonna House

ONE SUMMER DAY IN 1967, A CZECH BENEDICTINE missionary from Africa unexpectedly arrived at our Mission House in Montreal. Father Vojtěch Vít, O.S.B., was relocating from the African Congo to Chicago. He knew about Madonna House, located in the hamlet of Combermere, Ontario. He wanted to visit the house, but I didn't know anything about it. I found the small village on a map, borrowed Father Dostál's car and off we went.

Properly dressed with Roman collars, we arrived at Combermere just before noon. Both of us were welcomed and invited for lunch with the large community. To our surprise, there were about ten other visiting priests in their clerical outfits at lunch tables in the big dining room that served several purposes. An atmosphere of gentle excitement and expectation filled the room. When we asked what it was about, we were told that Bea, the Russian founder of the House, was about to arrive. She had been away for several days and was expected to report to the community on her adventures.

Soon Bea, a heavy set, commanding woman with a big smile, appeared. Everybody became silent. She had been at the Canadian Bishops Conference as a lay advisor. Bea briefly described the concerns and serious practical problems of the bishops that seemed to have no acceptable solutions. As she spoke in proper English with a heavy Russian accent, she turned to the assembled priests with teasing and challenging words: "So, Reverend Fathers, you wise theologians, what would you do? What would be your advice to your bishops?"

There was silence. Nobody spoke.

"Speak up you learned men," she continued.

I felt embarrassed … not so much by her teasing words, but for the silence of the large group of priests. Nobody dared to say anything. I raised my hand and said, "In such a difficult situation that doesn't seem to have a reasonable solution, I don't see any other way than prayer and calm, trust in our Heavenly Father. After all, we are His children."

Bea exploded. "Yes! That's it! That's the answer!"

We clerics were saved from embarrassment in front of the large lay community of the house. I started to like Bea—quite an authentic, sincere, courageous and intelligent character. One would not dare play games with her.

Several years later when Vera and I were married, I toyed with the idea of joining this open-minded, spiritual community at the Madonna House as a couple. I took Vera to Combermere and introduced her to Bea. When Bea heard that Vera was a social worker, she snapped. "Those social workers in their expensive fur coats among the poorest people! What do they know or understand?"

Vera felt insulted, and her reaction, expressed only to me, was, "What does she know about what we're doing? She shouldn't generalize like that." That was the end of Madonna House for us. Vera, a highly compassionate social worker with an excellent reputation who would work overtime for her clients late into the night, would not consider living in Combermere. However, Vera was a forgiving person who soon forgot about the incident.

After Vera became a Roman Catholic, we returned to Madonna House. On several occasions we stayed there overnight, often separated from each other in their hermitages. Other times I went there alone.

On one occasion, Bea addressed me in front of a group of the residents in the house. "Who are you? Are you a psychiatrist or what? We need a good psychiatrist over here," she said.

"I'm not a psychiatrist," I replied. "I am a priest, but no longer a cleric, because I got married." She stepped forward, took both my hands and kissed them in front of everybody. I felt uncomfortable, but I had to accept it. Later when I came for an overnight visit, they accommodated me in their special house for priests where there was a chapel with the Blessed Sacrament. The staff did this not knowing my background … or did they? I do not know.

On another occasion when I was there without Vera, all the dinner tables were pushed towards the walls after supper and a circle (called kolo) dance began. Everyone held hands, moved one way, and then the opposite way, and on and on. Bea was dancing too. No one was forced to dance. I stood in a corner observing what was happening. After a while, Bea broke out of the kolo dance and came over to me.

"You see," she said, "this is very important. We have striving and searching people here who cannot understand philosophical and theological speculations, speeches, and arguments. But they do understand something else that philosophers have a hard time understanding or accepting. Such little souls need and enjoy human touch and down to earth activities. Watch them. Aren't they beautiful? Simple enjoyment is important." She then rejoined the dancers.

When Vera and I settled in Mississauga, she had to commute to downtown Toronto where she worked for the Protestant Metropolitan Children's Aid Society. I decided to buy her a good second hand car. We then had two cars, with one sitting in our garage because she didn't want it. The commuter train was good enough for her. One winter day I had the idea to give Vera's car to Madonna House, as they certainly could use it. Vera had no objections.

On the following Saturday she drove one car and I followed her with the other to Madonna House. When we arrived, we were accepted with a joyful commotion in the community. I asked what all the excitement was about, and they explained that they only had two old cars, a

Jeep and a passenger car. A few days earlier, one of their priests had wrecked the passenger car in an accident. Now they were stuck and didn't know how to solve the problem because they had no money for another car. On Bea's advice, the whole community started to pray for a car. Within three days Vera's car arrived as a gift. Vera and I felt happy about it. I encourage you to learn more about Madonna House.[8]

39. Reflections on Love

To THE TOMES THAT HAVE BEEN WRITTEN ABOUT love, particularly romantic love, I reluctantly add my experiences and views.

I believe in love! I have experienced its depths, its joys and its cruelty ... cruelty rooted in the self-centredness of erotic love with which most mature adults are familiar in varying degrees.

It is a Christian belief that God is a creative Person whose essence is of Living Love. He is not a mechanical sea of love of which all people and all creatures are little love droplets, as understood in the monistic philosophical and religious systems. God is a Self-Giver, Perfection, Beauty, Truth, Humility, Understanding, Unity and a Saviour incarnated into humanity in the Jewish person of Jesus Christ. He/She is the One, the real Life. Every one of us is consciously or unconsciously thirsting for Him/Her.

Unfortunately, a great part of modern humanity has become lost in rationalism, skepticism, or ignorance of the Divine Invisible and Intangible Reality. Polytheistic religious systems explain reality as consisting of many very powerful or less powerful gods, spiritual living beings who control everything, outhouses included. This

JIŘÍ (GEORGE) HOŘÁK

view is often full of superstitions. It is radically rejected in Judeo-Christian tradition.

I am aware that what I'm saying appears to be nonsense to a strictly rational mind rooted in observation and measurements of material dimensions of reality. It is nonsense to a rationalistic mind in which intuition became subordinated or totally ignored by the analytic and logical mind. It is a refined and disciplined intuition that leads open-minded individuals, like true artists and mystics, beyond the tangible, strictly logical dimensions of our human existence.

Spoken or written language alone is inadequate to express in a rational and logical fashion the heat, the fire, the flame, the silence, the pain, the joy and the pleasure of the unifying Living Love. Poetry and classical music come closest.

Usually when people use the word "love," they mean Eros. Sex is an expression of life-giving love on the biological level; however, man is not only biology. In higher forms of love, eroticism inevitably changes into a stronger experience of the uniting energy of love. With this form of love, material separation and distance do not break the union of mature lovers. Their union is one living flame that blazes beyond the grave.

Motherly and fatherly love is a higher, less self-centred form of self-giving than a merely erotic, sexual love. The love of family, love of the clan or nation, love of friends, and up the scale to the love of humanity, beauty, truth, and harmony all surpass a simple, physical love. Even higher is the love of all-encompassing unity, the love of God, and in God the love of everybody and everything, even of the horrible, redeeming, cleansing pain.

This is what true religion is about. St. Paul's Hymn on Love (1 Corinthians 13:1–13) is a revelation of the infinite depths of the Living Mystery. If our heart wants to understand it, then it has to move beyond logic and the analytic ability of our ordinary mind; we need to get on our knees, breathe, and keep silent.

On a more practical and comprehensible level, I accept Antoine de Saint-Exupéry's description of true love: "Love does not consist in gazing at each other but in looking outward together in the same direction."[9] This insightful statement is also correct theologically.[10] Trying to look forward in the same direction unites ... even with God! Looking forward in the same direction is an ongoing experience of mutual trust and sharing. Mistakes and errors don't break the unity. That "looking together in the same direction" becomes a form of prayer, contemplative prayer in which we might perceive the luminescence of the invisible God who is the loving Father of Jesus Christ and of us all.

On the more human level, this experience is expressed in the joyful and beautifully explosive "Alleluia, Alleluia!" of Handel and other composers and poets.

40. Surprise and Conflict

I HAVE EXPLAINED MY UNDERSTANDING AND IDEAL of love, an ideal I had been striving for in my religious life. Now I have to tackle my explosion of love towards a living, human person, an intelligent and attractive young woman. I feel love for her to this very day.

When I started school at the age of six, I liked a beautiful girl in my first grade class. I imagined being with her, touching her and sleeping with her. Of course, I didn't know what it all was about. My innate curiosity was behind my inquisitive questions to my mother: What makes a girl a girl? Why am I a boy? Why does she have long hair and my hair is short? Why do the girls and boys have separate bathrooms at school? My questions were not answered, except for with a loving smile.

My first description of sexual activity took place when I was hospitalized at the age of eleven. A boy in the bed next to mine described his parents having sexual intercourse in graphic language. I was disgusted. *My parents would never do such a thing*, I thought. When his parents came to visit him, I avoided them.

At the age of twelve, I was introduced to masturbation by other boys and I practiced it until I was eighteen, when at my first religious retreat I learned about its negative aspects and its sinfulness. Since then, I stopped it entirely. Prayer, having other concerns, and always being busy and responsible for something helped me in this regard. I found the self-discipline helpful in other areas also.

When I was fifteen, two older fellow apprentices at work told me about their fun with girls when they were introducing them to intercourse. They told me about pregnancies and abortions of which I knew nothing. I felt ignorant and curious at the same time. They showed me illegal pornographic literature and told me where to get it. I never did, but I have seen some of it.

Much later, at the age of twenty-one, one of my older friends, the father of two little boys, told me that when his boys were older, he would teach them about sex by taking them to a brothel. The girls there would educate them properly. Meanwhile, he was sending his boys to a private Catholic school to get a good education from the nuns. That scandalized me and hurt me, but I couldn't change it. I had to accept it and adjust accordingly to this perverse reality of "nice" and respectable people who were my friends.

After the age of eighteen, I wasn't interested in learning more about sexual matters. I didn't feel that I was missing out on anything. I accepted that sex was something exciting and important, yet there was something more important and beautiful than a gross sexual lifestyle. That attitude evolved from my first religious retreat and in subsequent religious training in asceticism. I observed the differences among people, whether men or women, the differences in their social and psychological backgrounds, and in their childhood upbringing. It explained much of their behaviour and made them acceptable, even if I felt unpleasant and even irritated by their views.

My parents didn't know anything about my education on the street. Sex remained taboo in our family. To speak about it was considered sinful and had to be confessed and absolved in the confessional. Much later, even as a priest, I didn't know about the differences between male and female sexual experiences and preferences. I was quite skillful at suppressing and rationalizing my sexual feelings and inclinations without ever avoiding women. I always liked them; I liked their company and felt comfortable with them in spite of the sexual barrier that I built. I was aware of homosexuality and lesbianism, but didn't pay it much attention. In my mind, it was simply human weakness, aberration and perversion.

Later in life, I learned about sexual masochism, sadistic perversion and bestiality, particularly when I was as a student chaplain in a psychiatric hospital and while working in the criminal system. With my previous ignorance of all the ramifications of sexuality and the negative social consequences of its use and abuse, I had not missed much. Actually, my past ignorance made my private life easier. Gradually I became well equipped to deal with the public, but I was dry inside, ready to be set on fire. I had the tendency to be judgmental rather than compassionate. So much for my public confession.

When Father Felix M. Davídek introduced me to some classic world literature, I enjoyed the story of Don Quixote de la Mancha and his Dulcinea. What impressed me most in this story was how the intelligent Dulcinea thought she knew who she was ... namely a gypsy, a rough prostitute ... and how under the influence of the crazy Don Quixote she changed into a noble lady through the idealistic manner that Don Quixote perceived her. She needed a crazy man like Don Quixote to discover who she really was as a human being: a real beauty, a lady.

Petronila was different. Her intellectual ability, her beauty, her smile and her knowledge of Catholic clergy's private problems impressed me deeply. I saw in her more than she saw in herself. We connected and I became an infatuated teenager. A deep, inner conflict was born in me. The more I tried to get her out of my mind and my life, the more she was settling in my heart.

She understood me well, better than I understood myself. She sensed that I was trying to get rid of her because she was a woman. It was childish and unacceptable to her. She felt our relationship was incomplete and unhealthy. I could see it and believe it, yet I was stubborn; I had my vows. I needed the situation resolved or I would become mentally sick and probably suffer an emotional breakdown.

In the fall of 1967, she came back to visit me in Toronto. She accompanied me in my car from Toronto to Cleveland and back to Toronto. Her presence and her ongoing excited chatting made me very happy, but at the same time very anxious. I didn't know what to do. I became internally torn. In her presence I was a happy, but helpless little boy. I tried to teach her, but really she was teaching me how to see life from a feminine perspective. I appreciated it.

She returned again in the spring of 1968 under the pretense of buying a new car in Toronto. We travelled for two days in her car as far as Sault Ste. Marie, Ontario. There she bought me an airfare ticket back to Toronto because I had no money. It was a humbling experience for me. If anything, it was I who should have paid for her. I was intoxicated with her, but at the same time I experienced periods of deep anger toward her. I felt that she was controlling me. In a way I liked it even when I was angry with her. I was confused. I kept telling her again and again that she must get married. She refused to listen, telling me that she would never get married.

In spite of my erotic intoxication and craziness, I managed somehow to carry on with my duties and maintain a decent external behaviour. There was no effective spiritual guidance available to me except the understanding admonishments in the confessional that I would give as a priest to someone else in a similar life situation.

I spoke openly to my provincial Father McDougall about my emotional involvement with a woman and my troublesome state of mind. He sent me for relaxation to a Jesuit villa at Lake Joseph. There I spoke about the chaotic state of my soul to an old Jesuit priest who was in charge of the villa. He was understanding ... not counselling or arguing ... just accepting. His kind and calm listening was supportive and helpful in dealing with my inner pain, but did not resolve it.

Petronila somehow learned my whereabouts. She phoned me and invited me to her wedding. She just did what I was telling her to do for the sake of my priestly vocation, yet I felt like I was being stabbed in the back.

My social behaviour was focused on my good manners for the purpose of covering up my inner chaos. I managed my sorrowful emotional and mental state with the help of prayer and with the daily practice of hatha yoga, sometimes two or three sessions per day. The daily celebration of the Holy Mass and my praying for Petronila and her fiancé were a great help. In spite of my mistakes, I was faithful to my vows. Petronila had to be sacrificed. I loved her dearly, but vows were vows. I will be able to say to God at my judgment, "I kept my vows; I am not like those who broke them."

The wedding day arrived. With the approval of my well informed provincial, I drove nonstop several thousand kilometres west. When I arrived at her city, I settled in a Jesuit community, had a hot bath and went to sleep. I was exhausted.

The next evening was the pre-wedding party at her parents' house. I got a ride with some Jesuits who were also attending the party. When we arrived in our clerical outfits, she stepped forward in front of everybody, including her parents and her bridegroom, gave me a big hug, and kissed me on the lips. More physical embraces followed, expressing our passionate love.

Our drama culminated in a well rehearsed marriage ceremony. I stood at the altar with other priests dressed in our priestly robes; the church was packed and she walked all alone in her bridal dress to meet her bridegroom at the altar. Nobody, except the two of us, and possibly her bridegroom and a few of her closest friends, knew what was taking place. The performance for the public was flawless—even on my part.

Petronila is now an old woman living in Texas. I never stopped loving her with a higher love than mere erotic love. I appreciated what her husband did for my priestly vocation by marrying her. How much he knew about my love for her, I don't know. Probably he did know. He died of Parkinson's disease.

In retrospect, I think that Petronila as a younger, intelligent wife with high expectations would have shredded me emotionally because of my naiveté, my guilt feelings and my economic inadequacy. Except for those visits,

I've respectfully kept away from her and her family all these years.

41. Return to Montreal

ON MY RETURN JOURNEY TO MONTREAL, I STAYED overnight with Father Křivánek, a Czech parish priest in rural Manitoba. He invited me to accompany him for an evening visit with a farm family. They had given him an expensive hunting rifle for his birthday and he was paying a visit to express his appreciation. I gladly went with him.

When we arrived at the farm, there was great joy and excitement.

"Father is here, Father is here," the children yelled. There were six or seven children, the oldest no more than fifteen. In the joy and excitement, nobody paid attention to me. I stood silently in the corner of the room, observing what was happening.

At my feet on the floor was a little girl quietly playing with her dolls, oblivious to the commotion. *Here is my company*, I thought, sitting down to join her at play. I assisted her with putting her dolls to bed for a good night's sleep by covering them with small blankets. I asked her about each doll and she told me their names, and she described the furniture in her little playhouse.

We had fun; there was an easy, sweet communication between us. She spoke in clear sentences and with good pronunciation to me, a stranger.

Suddenly there was silence in the room and we were surrounded by the whole family. From my position on the floor, I asked what was going on. The oldest daughter spoke up, explaining with a voice full of wonder, "Nobody has ever heard her to say a word. This is a miracle. She can speak!" Astonished, I looked at the joyful faces around me and at my little friend sitting beside me on the floor. Among the happy faces was a pair of angry eyes—her mother's.

Back on the road again the next day, I felt emotionally sick and tired. When I arrived at our Mission House in Montreal, I had mixed feelings and couldn't stop thinking about the woman I loved who had just married at my urging. I couldn't stop my crying heart. I was emotionally helpless, powerless. On top of it all, I found out that my father had died at the time of the wedding. Deep down I cared about him and thought that I understood him well. The last time I had seen him was at the small railroad station in Navojná, eighteen years earlier.

It would be difficult to describe our Jesuit group as a real religious community. Its founder, Father Feřt, went back to Rome. Father Kovanda, our new superior, was spending most of his time in Texas. Brother Waligora went to a restaurant every evening to wash dishes and kept his meagre income for himself. Father Lang kept borrowing money from a trusting French family, but he did not repay the money. As a dependent religious, he had no right borrowing it. It was unacceptable behaviour for which he would have been dismissed from the Jesuits under normal circumstances. But our circumstances were not normal.

Father Pelikán wanted me to come to California because he was old and would be retiring soon. I wanted go. In my emotional state, I needed to get involved with ordinary people; however the order came from distant Rome that Father Popelka was to replace Father Pelikán Old Father Dostál came and went according to his personal agenda and could not be counted on. The only stable man was Father Janíček whose priority seemed to be Hostýn, his children's camp. He was a practical man of few words. He was ten years my senior, and I found it difficult to have a real discussion with him. He controlled the finances of our house.

There was no future for me in the Czech Mission House. I was the youngest member of that group, a member who had not completed the customary third probation. All the members of our Jesuit group were good men, but somehow because of the political and economic circumstances of the world, too often they were left on their own and became strong individualists, not easily managed.

I, the naive idealist, went to see Father McDougall in Toronto, the head of the English speaking Jesuit Province in which territory we were located. I discussed our problems with him. I was surprised when he appointed me the new superior of our Czech Mission House. For him, it was a diplomatic way out of a situation he didn't know how to resolve. He gave me complete juridical power that allowed me a free hand to make decisions concerning our Mission House and its members. At the same time, he left the official title of superior to Father Kovanda because of his fragile emotional state. He did not want to hurt him.

42. Montreal to Toronto

ARMED WITH THE POWERS OF MY APPOINTMENT AS the superior of the Czech Mission House, I felt that my first step in attempting to make our group of Jesuits function more like a community was to find out the financial state of our house. I had to know our monthly income and its source, and our monthly expenses. After all, on the practical level we were living in poverty. All the members of our group were frugal, except perhaps Father Lang, but even his personal expenses were more for his group of Montreal artists than for himself.

I understood that the bank account of our house was at the west end Bank of Montreal. I went to the bank, introduced myself as the new superior of the Czech Mission House, and asked to see our bank account. I was referred to the manager. I told him who I was and that I needed to see the Czech Mission House account. He did not waste words.

"There is no Czech Mission House account here," he said. "The only account we have is the private account of Father Janíček. You have no right to see somebody else's private account."

I felt embarrassed, ignorant and stupid. I pondered our situation. So, it has been Father Janíček who had the real control of our house affairs. Putting our finances in his hands had allowed him to manipulate the income and the expenses of our house to meet the needs of Camp Hostýn, according to his judgment. My previous two superiors, Father Feřt and Father Kovanda, were new to Canada. Not knowing the Canadian legal administrative practices regarding insurance, taxes and banking, they depended on Father Janíček. Father Janíček could do as he pleased, yet he was not an irresponsible man.

It was not a good situation. To get into an argument with Father Janíček, who had the support of the Montreal Czech and Slovak immigrant parishioners and also his camp Hostýn collaborators, would be fruitless. It would be a poor strategy. He had worked hard, but not for himself; he was doing what he loved to do. The best plan seemed to be to let things continue, not to interfere, not to rock the boat. Asserting my role as the superior might be right, but it would be destructive rather than constructive.

I returned to Toronto and reported my analysis of our Mission House situation to the provincial. I also submitted my resignation as the legal superior. The provincial accepted it and asked me what I wanted to do. I said that besides my basic priesthood duties, I would like to specialize in clinical psychology. That was fine with him, but he explained that becoming a fully qualified clinical psychologist would take years of study and a lot of money— money from my own pocket. After all, the Czech Jesuits were only guests in his province and his province had its own expenses. Then he made an interesting offer.

One of his young priests had started a full-time course dealing with professional chaplaincy in hospitals and correctional institutions. After he graduated and received his professional chaplaincy certificate, he would be placed in a paid position in one of the government institutions. That priest had quit the course because he found it too difficult; he couldn't stomach the training because the inquisitive and intensive sensitivity training was too much for him. If I wished, I could take his place in the course. After I graduated from the course and was in a good position, I could register for the clinical psychology studies. I accepted the provincial's offer without hesitation.

The course was offered at the Queen Street Mental Health Centre in Toronto in co-operation with the professional medical hospital staff. The director of the course was Bert, an Anglican priest. I went to see Bert and had a long talk with him. I revealed to him, priest to priest, my relationship with Petronila. I told him about her marriage and about my being in an emotionally disturbed state of mind in which I was unable to stop thinking about her. I assumed sharing my intimate feelings with him would be kept confidential. Bert accepted me into the course and the provincial arranged for my accommodation in a Jesuit residence in Toronto. The expenses for my accommodation and the course would be covered by his province.

There were only two students in the full time course— Doug, a United Church minister, and Vera, a social worker from the Metropolitan United Church.

During our first group meeting, Bert introduced me as a Jesuit and then opened the session with a question directed at me.

"George, tell us as you told me about your affairs with women."

My trust in his confidentiality was broken at once. I felt stabbed in the back, embarrassed and angry. A Catholic priest and a Jesuit accused of having affairs with women! That was not true, except for my love for Petronila. Accused of affairs with women in front of two non-Catholics whom I did not know! That was a straight attack not only on me, but also on the Catholic priesthood. I had to deal with it on the spot in a diplomatic way without exploding. Somehow I kept my anger under control.

After about two months, I realized that Bert was a bright, talented man, but under the surface he was hostile with unresolved personal problems. He did not like me, yet he tolerated me; we got along okay, I thought. In the sensitivity group, he labelled me a skillful fencer with words who sneaks out of every emotional confrontation. That was not the way I felt about myself. I thought I was transparent and honest.

I started the course at the end of September. In November, another Bert, a Passionist Catholic priest from Nova Scotia, joined us. He was calm, easy going, and had a good sense of humour; he was an asset to our intense sensitivity group. Shortly before Christmas, Bert, our director and leader, openly told to me he didn't want me in the course any longer. He even wrote a negative report about me to the provincial. In the report, he set up a condition that I would only be allowed in the course if I passed a psychiatric examination that he would set up. I accepted that condition and so did the provincial.

My examination was conducted by the head psychiatrist of the Clark Institute, a reputable psychiatric institute in Toronto. I received a phone call from the institute for a two o'clock appointment. When I met the psychiatrist, I explained to him why I was there and told him to feel free to ask any question because I had no problem being transparent after the many confessions I'd made in my life.

The doctor started the interview, digging deeper and deeper into my soul. After about thirty minutes, he called his receptionist and asked her to cancel the next appointment because he needed more than an hour with me.

The interview lasted two hours, but the conclusion was a pleasant surprise.

"If I have ever met a mentally and emotionally healthy person at this place, it's you," he said. "That you're upset under your circumstances is normal. If you weren't disturbed, I'd be worried about you. You have been able to deal with a very difficult emotional situation with your own resources. I don't think you need to come back again. If you feel that you're no longer able to cope emotionally, phone me, and I'll prescribe medication. It's not you who should be sitting in this chair, but your supervisor ... but he would never come or listen."

I was allowed to continue the course. After Bert received the report from the psychiatrist, he began to respect me. My resources were simple: prayer, Holy Mass and daily practice of hatha yoga. In emotionally tense situations, I would breathe deeply and stand on my head for twenty or more minutes, sometimes three times a day.

43. Chaplain in Psychiatry

THE QUEEN STREET MENTAL HEALTH CENTRE IS the largest psychiatric hospital in Toronto. It was opened under the name of Lunaticum in 1850. The hospital once served as a training ground for medical doctors moving into psychiatry. As a full time chaplaincy student, I was well accepted by the psychiatric professional staff, particularly by Professor Dr. Miller, the head of the psychiatric staff, and his counterpart, Professor Mallow, an experienced, older female psychiatrist.

On several occasions, I spent time in the private offices of Dr. Miller and Dr. Mallow discussing philosophic theories and practical approaches to psychiatric problems. They trusted me and assigned me as a therapist to several patients who had been in the hospital for a long time without showing signs of improvement. Probably in their opinion, I could not do any harm. It would be difficult to make these patients worse off than they already were. I was given a master key to all locked wards and to the main administration building. I could move around as I pleased. That was in October, 1968.

In my zeal and also in my emotional need to get involved with people, I spent time in the hospital and with the patients, not only during the assigned day shifts, but also beyond those times, and sometimes at nights. I loved my new occupation and the trust given to me by my new teachers. Files of all patients were open to me and I studied them often. It was my curiosity that guided me as well as my need to keep busy with other people's problems.

Three examples from my therapeutic work with difficult or permanent patients will provide a snapshot of my experience in the psychiatric hospital.

One case involved a middle-aged Portuguese fellow who behaved as a seriously depressed and disoriented person. He spoke only in a very low whisper, so everybody had difficulty hearing what he was saying. Medication and group therapy were not working for him. Professor Mallow asked me to look after him. I accepted the challenge and then I figured out what approach I would take with him. What interested me was the fact that the eyes of this simple man were not always withdrawn, but were sometimes alive and observant of what was happening around him.

For his therapy I needed a large, quiet space. I requested the key to the hospital gym and took him there. Nobody else was around. I asked the patient a simple question, and as usual, he whispered something that I couldn't hear or understand. I put my hands to my ears and told him in a friendly, commanding voice to repeat what he had said in a loud voice. He tried to please me, but without much improvement. Again I asked the same question with the same gesture and a smile, insisting on his answer. His reply was a bit louder, but not much. So we continued repeating the childish game again and again. Finally, his whisper started to change into a voice. Then we came to the point that I was moving step by step away from him and requesting that he speak louder and louder. The therapy session changed into a comedy game. Finally, I was at the other end of the gym. He shouted at me with a good, solid voice. Then he burst into a big, noisy laugh. And I did too. We started to talk normally. His English was amazingly good.

The patient had been raised somewhere in the hill country of Portugal. He had immigrated to Canada because his sister was living here. Once in Canada, he was left on his own and had no real friends. He worked hard and saved money, but someone cheated him of his savings. He lost his trust in people and started to withdraw. Bitter, he didn't want to speak to anybody. He became a lost and disoriented soul and landed in the psychiatric hospital. There his case was assigned to a young woman doctor. That was it—the woman doctor was the reason for his permanent withdrawal.

"They think that I'm crazy and keep telling me that that woman is my doctor," he said. "I'm not so crazy as to believe it."

I confirmed that indeed she was a doctor and that in Canada it was possible.

"She can't be a doctor ... she is a woman," he insisted.

I realized that the root of his emotional problem was cultural and the assignment of a female doctor reinforced his distrust. In his opinion, I was a doctor. Rather than medication, he needed a bit of understanding and re-education. Through our comedy therapy, he started to trust me. In several days, he was referred to the social work department and released from the hospital. Professor Mallow smiled and assigned me to another apparently hopeless case.

A middle-aged female patient was locked in a ward, her psychiatric treatment going nowhere. I checked her file and realized that she was not stupid. I thought the first thing to do would be to get her naturally relaxed and then develop a trusting relationship with her. I asked the nurses for an empty room and two blankets. They told her to meet me the next day, lightly dressed in her pants and t-shirt without her bra. I wanted to teach her to practice the yoganada relaxation technique on the floor. I put on short pants under my ordinary black pants.

When she arrived the next day, she watched with interest while I spread the two blankets on the floor and then took off my pants. She let out a great sigh, exclaiming, "I haven't seen a man take off his pants for such a long time!" That was it! She'd had enough of being restricted in the hospital. Professor Mallow had a big laugh when she heard what had happened. My dear patient was referred to the social work department and left the hospital in a few days.

The third story was more serious. Once a month, professional staff held an educational information day in
the hospital amphitheater. The chaplaincy department
was asked to make a presentation about their work in the
hospital. I volunteered for our department. The focus of
my presentation was on the more practical rather than
theoretical, therapeutic approach to patients.

There I was, confidently facing doctors, psychologists, social workers and nurses. As my example, I
selected Anna, a middle-aged female patient who had
been hospitalized in a closed ward for several years.
Anna was a simple woman, an immigrant from Hungary
with a limited knowledge of English, abandoned by her
husband. She had suffered enormously with ongoing
fear and anxiety. She was one of the hopeless cases for
whom nothing worked: not medication, not electroshock
therapy, not lobotomy. Day and night she held her rosary
in her hand, hanging on to it for dear life. Her symptoms
were simple and always the same.

I started to pay attention to Anna on a daily basis.
There was an evil man in her imagination who frightened
her and was going to kill her. Trying to convince her
otherwise with logical reasoning didn't work. Day after
day she told me that she would be dead the next time I
came to see her. Sometimes she interrupted our simple
conversation by telling me with a trembling voice, "He is
here; he is here!" She would then become very agitated.

After I described the case, a nurse dressed in her professional uniform (not normally used in the hospital) brought Anna into the theatre. Professor Miller approached me and offered his help in front of the large audience.

"George, this is too difficult," he said. "Let me handle the interview with Anna.

I declined his offer, explaining that because I had established a relationship with Anna, she would talk to me, while he with his skills might not succeed because he did not have a relationship with her.

My interview with Anna turned out well. At once she recognized me on this foreign stage and related with me beautifully. Of course, there was no healing in the performance; it was just a show.

It seems that very few people, particularly younger people, realize how much mental and emotional anguish exists in our modern society. Faith and responsible religion with its trust, prayers and devotions, can alleviate much of it.

44. Vera

I FIRST MET VERA IN A SENSITIVITY GROUP OF four. I felt uneasy in her presence, although I knew nothing about her except that she was older than I and was a Protestant. Being a celibate priest in a boundary-less sensitivity group with a woman, a Protestant minister and an Anglican priest, made me quite uncomfortable. No wonder the young Jesuit priest had quit the group. I would have preferred a men's group, preferably composed of Catholic men. But there she was, and I had no intention of backing out and quitting the course. I was polite with Vera, but not very friendly.

For eight months we had three ninety-minute sensitivity sessions per week. Gradually I adjusted to the group and the intensity didn't bother me any longer. Everyone's behaviour was analyzed under a microscope. Sometimes it was quite entertaining. I couldn't avoid Vera in our interaction, just as she couldn't avoid me. Her gentle manners and her reluctance to express her views and opinions fascinated me; when she voiced her views, they were to the point and precise. I started to think that under her quiet surface, she was a deep thinker.

After about a month, the chaplaincy was asked to have a religious service at the hospital for staff and patients.

Vera volunteered to accept responsibility for it, and I became curious about what this Protestant woman would do. I came to the service as an observer rather than a participant. I was impressed. There she was, well prepared, competent, nothing doctrinally wrong in her sermon, communicating with the congregation quietly with her eyes and body language. The congregation was captivated and listened attentively to what she was saying.

It was a surprise for me. I realized that I was prejudiced against her as a woman and also as a Protestant. I started to pay more attention to her, observing her in a friendly manner. This woman had something to offer, but what was it? She was emotionally blocked and repressed under her pleasant social manners; I thought she was in some kind of a trouble and needed help.

In the sensitivity group, she disclosed that she had difficulty operating in the closed psychiatry ward assigned to her. She had problems communicating with the patients and didn't feel comfortable with the staff. I felt quite competent in my ward, so I occasionally stopped by her ward to assist and encourage her. I started to play therapist to her. Assisting her seemed to have a healing impact on my unresolved and emotionally disturbing relationship with Petronila, who was now married.

One Saturday afternoon towards the end of November of 1968, the Jesuit community at 2 Dale Avenue in Toronto dispersed, heading off to visit their families and friends. The community car was available to me, so I phoned Vera and asked what she was doing.

"Nothing," she answered in a low, depressed voice.

I asked her whether she would keep me company driving to Niagara Falls, and she agreed.

On the way to Niagara Falls, she sat beside me in the car like a clay statue, not saying a word. I tried to start a conversation with her several times without success. I thought I would try using body language by putting my hand on her cold, lifeless hand. I had no sinister intentions or thoughts ... I was just trying to reach her. There was no reaction, nothing, just complete withdrawal.

The city of Niagara Falls seemed to be abandoned—no tourists, and everything was closed down. Silently, we watched the falls for awhile and then found a nearly deserted restaurant where we had a coffee in silence.

When we returned to the car, we discovered that the keys were locked in it, but fortunately the driver's seat window was open a few inches. Nobody was around to help us, so we were in trouble. Suddenly, Vera came alive.

"I know what to do," she said. "In the restaurant, I saw wire coat hangers. Let's go back, get one of them and use it to open the door."

And that's what we did. The impractical Vera, biting her tongue and lips while maneuvering the coat hanger, managed to open the door. Success! What satisfaction!

Things changed on the way back to Toronto. She was chatting away, confiding that she was emotionally sick.

Life was empty for her and didn't make much sense. It was going nowhere. She'd tried therapy with a private psychologist, but had quit after seven sessions because it was useless. Then she tried again with Bert, our Anglican priest supervisor, but the results were the same. Nothing was coming of it. She invited me to her apartment which was a mess. I helped her to bring it into some kind of manageable order and then left.

At the psychiatric hospital she started to relate to me differently, more openly, and with a little smile ... more than just friendly. My interaction with this woman was helping me to deal with the pain in my heart over my previous loss. I did not experience the slightest trace of erotic inclination towards Vera. We became good friends and that was all. We developed a healthy, mature, mutually trusting relationship.

At the Christmas holidays, our sensitivity group dispersed, as did the residents of our Jesuit community house. Only one brother and another priest remained. Vera went home to her mother and her brother's family in Grand Falls, Newfoundland. She planned to be back in Toronto on January 3rd to continue with our residential chaplaincy course.

It was late in the evening of Christmas day. I was in my room, alone and lonely. Nobody was home. I kept praying and half dreaming about past Christmases, particularly Christmases of my childhood, and meditating on the divine incarnation. My room was in darkness with a little candle burning in front of a small nativity scene. Suddenly, out of the blue, a clear message came to me.

"Vera is back from Newfoundland. She's in Toronto, and she's desperate."

What nonsense, I thought.

"Oh yes, she is back and she's in a serious trouble!"

You're hallucinating in your loneliness, my brain reasoned.

"Phone her and you'll see," the inner voice continued.

"That's a good idea," I replied. That would clear the obsessive thought.

I called, not expecting anyone to answer, but at the other end of the line I heard a weak voice. "Yes. Yes, I am in Toronto."

I asked her what had happened. "I want to see you," I said. "Wait for me at the corner by the Presbyterian church. I'll be there in fifteen minutes."

She was waiting for me. It was midnight. I took her to an Oriental restaurant on Yonge Street and asked her why she had not stayed in Newfoundland on such a festive day. We had a good time at the restaurant, but the situation was not funny at all. Vera revealed that she had to run away from her family and from Newfoundland because she could no longer resist her suicidal drive to walk into the cold sea.

That Christmas episode put me into a new emotional state that no one knew about. This beautiful, intelligent, well educated woman was becoming more and more attached to me. I hoped I would be able to handle it somehow, but I didn't know how. I was resolved to stick to my religious vows. I valued Vera's friendship, her trust in me, and her femininity, yet with a kind of horror, I realized that I was sliding into a similar situation as with Petronila. At this stage, there were two women in my heart, both very different from each other, yet I cared about both of them. Vera gradually became a hot wire that I had to resolve, but I didn't know how. The problem of the meaning of love and self-centredness that culminated in a subtle form of my "holy" selfishness tortured my mind again. Definitely I did not want to marry Vera.

Spiritually I felt a bit like the Pharisee in Luke 18:10–14. "O God," I prayed, "I am not like the rest of men. I am a religious, a Jesuit who observes his vows and the Church laws and regulations. I am torn apart again because of a woman. I don't want to be a sinner and break my promises! Help! Please help!" The answer was a deafening silence.

I prayed and prayed and practiced hatha yoga and took hot baths to calm down. I stood on my head in an effort to remain calm and be able to cope with my duties without having a nervous breakdown. I was succeeding, but the inner pain, the price to be paid for avoiding a psychosis, was enormous.

I know that this sounds immature and ridiculous, but that's the way it was. It was beyond Vera's understanding. How could she understand it with her Protestant background? In my heart, I was all alone again, and God was silent. The professional help I sought from several priest- psychologists didn't help at all. They listened, they expressed their understanding and acceptance and that was all. By trying to rescue Vera from her terrible existential emptiness, I was placing myself in a similar emotionally dangerous situation. Vera could not help. She became a sweet burden for me without ever knowing it and I could not tell her.

45. Marriage

By EASTER WEEK OF 1969, VERA AND I HAD DEVEL-
oped a deep relationship based on our knowledge of each
other through our intense sensitivity training sessions.

I loved her beautiful, suffering soul—a generous, intelligent, self-giving and poetry loving soul emerging from
suicidal desperation. I could not let her perish. My tense
and almost psychotic disposition had to stop; otherwise I
would have to be committed to a psychiatric ward.

My prayers, my yoga practice, my jumping in and out
of a tub of hot water didn't resolve anything. My religious
vows! And those women! I had let them get too close to
me, but how could I do otherwise? I resisted, I tried hard,
but I did not succeed. I prayed fervently. "What about us
men?" I asked. Deep down, are we much different from
women? Not really. Our interests and lifestyles might be
different, but not much.

"What should I do?" This continued to be my prayer.
Finally, a clear answer came in a quiet, silent, firm inner
voice. It was not the answer I expected or wanted to hear.

"You are free!"

"I'm not asking to be free," I said. "I'm asking for
direction, to be told what to do."

"You are free," the inner voice replied. "You are at an intersection in your life. Whether you go to the right or the left, I'll be with you. But you are free to make your own decisions."

For the first time in my life, I realized the taste of real freedom. It is liberating, but also scary. "I don't want to be free. I want a decision made for me; I will obey."

"You are free," repeated the inner voice.

As I reflect on this experience, I realize that the freedom we chase in our modern world is superficial. I discovered the loving, humble, spiritually guided obedience speaking in my conscience. I hope I will always be able to listen and to hear. There is so much noise in me!

Yes, to hear and to discern—that's the root of Christian obedience. It's an obedience that respects our spiritual freedom, contrary to the professional military obedience practiced in the army and in all successful and powerful organizations. To obey because I want to obey is different than to obey because I am afraid to disobey. In the first case, I am a free child of God; in the second case, I am no longer God's image, but a frightened slave. In the first case there is peace and joy. In the second case, anxiety, fear, and evil have power over me. Christian obedience characterizes true spirituality.

Nothing was resolved, but an important inner light was shed on my existential situation. I had to make my own decisions, to move either to the left or to the right, to get married or stick to my religious vows and let Vera follow her dark destiny. Whether I moved to the left or to the right, whichever decision I made, it would have positive and negative consequences. About that I was clear.

If I went to the left and decided to marry, I would be labelled a traitor and a Judas. I would be misunderstood and rejected by my Catholic friends, by clergy, and maybe by my own family in Czechoslovakia. If I moved to the right, what would happen to Vera? My Catholic friends would praise me and see me as an example of faithfulness. I would be faithful to my vows before God and would expect God to reward me. I would be praying to Him like the Pharisee in the temple in Luke 18:10–13: "God, I have been faithful to my clerical vocation, and kept my religious vows. I am not like the Judases who betrayed your Church."

Of course, my inner struggle was beyond Vera's awareness and understanding. With her Protestant background, she thought that most clergy sooner or later married.

Emotionally I couldn't afford to continue with my inner conflict, yet I couldn't make a decision. Therefore, I set a deadline for my decision, and the deadline was Easter Sunday of 1969. Resurrection Sunday came and my decision was not made. Finally, I made it late in the afternoon: I was not going to abandon Vera, whatever the consequences might be. After all, God is love and my decision is rooted in love of God, not in erotic love. Erotic love would follow naturally if I allowed it and I would allow it. Yes, I would marry Vera!

My decision was made on the Sunday of the resurrection of our Lord. No ritual, no ceremony, no witnesses, no clerical approval. It was Vera and I before God. Both of us were baptized; therefore our marriage was sacramental. We would accept and submit to all external requirements of civil authorities and the Roman Catholic Church.

Vera couldn't understand it all and was not interested in the theoretical, ecclesiastic reasoning, and social implications of my decision. My hope was that the clarification and putting things into a proper social and ecclesiastical order would come in time. From now on, we had each other and could count on each other.

On Easter Monday, the inner voice unexpectedly and briefly spoke to me again. "What you have done is very beautiful." What reassurance!

I spoke to the provincial about my situation. He asked me whether my decision to be married was firm. After I said it was, he invited me for a coffee and we continued our conversation in a matter of fact manner. He informed me that the following week he had to fly to Rome. There he would arrange for my discharge from the Jesuit order. Tears rolled down my cheeks, but they didn't influence my decision. He explained that as a priest, I would be transferred to secular clergy under a diocesan bishop. My future bishop would very probably place me in some small remote community where I would not be able to cause much damage. This would not be acceptable to Vera or to me.

After the provincial returned from Rome, he provided me with an official letter of discharge from the order that would be necessary for my future bishop. On that occasion, his Sotius (that is his right hand in the administration of the province) told me that I had successfully passed the final exam of Philosophy and Theology in front of five Jesuit professors. For that I would normally deserve the Theology Doctorate title. However, I was not registered at the Regis College of the University of Toronto. My studies were conducted only within the Jesuit order because of the arrangement between the Czech Jesuit group in Montreal and the Canadian Jesuit Province. I was not aware of this arrangement. The Czech Jesuit House had no money to pay for me. Consequently, academically I had nothing in my hands except the two certificates from the Lateran Atheneum in Rome.

The next step was my application through the Toronto archdiocese to be released from my vows and my clerical status. I was told that it would take at least five years, if not ten, before I received permission from Rome to get married. Some priests, after two or three years of "living in sin," change their minds and return as clerics to their priestly ministry. With their penitential spirit, the Church gladly accepts them back, and many of them become good, faithful, and successful pastors. All that sounded reasonable and understandable to me from the administrative point of view.

The day of our formal civil marriage, October 7, 1969, the Feast of Our Lady of the Rosary, was a busy one. It started at 7:00 a.m. with my confession and Holy Mass celebrated by our friend Bert, a Passionist priest. He came with us to the city hall ceremony, which was followed by a special lunch at La Scala Restaurant. Our witnesses were Bert, our Anglican supervisor at the psychiatric hospital, his wife, and Doug, a United Church minister, with his wife, and Bert, the Catholic Passionist priest. What an ecumenical event! Vera was happy, and I pretended to be happy too, but in fact I felt deeply humiliated and uncomfortable. Why was I going through all this? Why? For love, for love alone!

The formalization of our marital relationship in the Roman Catholic Church took place one year later at a church in Willowdale, a suburb of Toronto. The Toronto archdiocese received notification from Rome that my marriage to Vera was approved. We were told to meet a priest lawyer in the sacristy of the church. The priest was a canon lawyer who had been educated in Rome. With his eyes and body language he silently despised me. With Vera, a Protestant, he was warm and courteous, which I appreciated. Except for the priest, there was nobody else present. We repeated our marital vows and signed the ecclesiastical papers with only the priest present. No document, no marriage certificate was given to us. Vera already knew that in some respects Catholics are strange people. She had been involved in adopting out children who were fathered by priests. In our formal ecclesiastical marriage, she co-operated gracefully for my sake.

Other humiliations followed. Vera's mother in Newfoundland, a Protestant, proudly announced to a Catholic priest who was a friend of the family that Vera had married a Catholic priest. He replied that he was very sorry for Vera. "As Judas priest has betrayed the priesthood and the Church," he said, "so he will betray Vera." My mother-in-law was upset and came to Toronto to meet the Judas who had trapped her only daughter. We liked each other at once. Mrs. Moore was reassured that everything was fine. She didn't know about the desperate emotional condition of her only child. As a mother, she was happy that her daughter had found a husband.

46. Consequences

As EXPECTED, NEGATIVE CONSEQUENCES RESULTED from our marriage. With a clerical collar on my neck, I passed the Professional Chaplaincy Certification in front of a panel of six Anglican and Protestant ministers. I became a professional institutional chaplain, but I could no longer be employed by the government. The Catholic Church did not recognize my marriage yet; therefore I couldn't operate as its chaplain. No chaplaincy, no income. The Jesuits at the Czech Mission House in Montreal were surprised and hurt by my move, and I was sorry for hurting them. After ten years with them, I received $120.00 to start my life anew in the world.

Vera had no money and kept borrowing money from her mother in Newfoundland. Her mother lent me $1,000 because $120 was peanuts. I miscalculated with the psychiatric hospital. I thought that I could get employment in the psychology department as a therapist. When I approached the chief psychologist, he told me that a year ago he would have hired me at once, but now he couldn't. He showed me a recent letter from the government instructing him to hire only PhD clinical psychologists because the universities were producing too many and they needed decent employment. Then he paid me a useless but consoling compliment: "I am sorry that I cannot hire you. I am hiring two new graduates. It will take me two years to bring them to your level, if I can manage to get them to your level at all."

With her qualifications Vera found employment easily with the Protestant Metropolitan Toronto Children's Aid Society. That was good news for both of us. Before we were married, I resided in my own modest room in a boarding house. I was poor again. Now, financially I depended on her. She asked me to move to her one-bedroom apartment.

In seeking employment, I submitted resumes to various companies. Only a few responded, but after the interviews they didn't hire me because they believed I was too old to be trained. One of my applications went to the Crippled Children's Society. They felt that I was too old to work with crippled children.

I got a job driving a taxi in Toronto with a second rate taxi company. It was a learning experience for me. I learned about the life of a large city during the day and during the night. I performed miserably—not with the cab, but with my knowledge of the city. I was ashamed of myself, and after a month or so I quit.

A week later the Crippled Children's Society head office called. They said they were having some problems at the children's summer camp they operated on the shores of Lake Erie. The camp was always run by university students under the direction of a qualified nurse.

This year they needed a mature man who would be able to get along with students and assist the nurse in her leadership. One of the students who had been assigned as a driver was using drugs and behaving irresponsibly. They had fired him and asked me to replace him. I did so gladly and moved to the camp. That job provided my first paycheque. At the closing party at the end of the summer, the nurse and the students carried me around the room on their shoulders, ignoring my kicking and protesting.

I was unemployed again. I decided to try my neglected bookbindery skills. I found a newspaper advertisement for a paper cutter. After sixteen years I stood at the same but updated German guillotine cutter that I knew well. Two men, the foreman and his German expert guillotine cutter, looked over my shoulder. They warned me that my job would be precision cutting of valuable material; seven applicants who had claimed they could do the job had failed. I passed and got the job with Visi Records, and with it a steady income. I started to feel better about myself, but it was not what I wanted to do. Deep down I wanted to continue to operate as a priest within the Catholic Church, but legally that wasn't possible. My second choice was working in a healing profession, specifically clinical psychology.

Vera made me an offer. She would support both of us and I could study psychology. She bought a new car, and we started to live reasonably well in her centrally located apartment.

I applied for graduate studies at York University, submitting my graduation documents from the Papal Atheneum Lateranense in Rome. My application was rejected. The university explained that the Papal Lateran University in Rome, according to the International Standard Evaluation of Universities around the world, operated on the level of a better high school, except for the faculty of law which was recognized as a university faculty. However, I was told if I had similar documents from the Gregorian University in Rome, I could be admitted to graduate studies. Then York University made a proposal. If I accumulated six credits on the undergraduate level, I could apply for admission to graduate studies in Clinical Psychology as a mature student. At the same time, I was warned that even then, I had very little chance of being accepted because each year there were very few openings for graduate clinical psychology studies and there were many younger applicants with top marks who were better qualified.

After Vera and I discussed our situation, I registered for undergraduate studies as a mature adult. I was forty years old. For a short time, I tried to cope with my employment and the studies at the same time, but soon I had to quit my job. It was too much for me.

47. Bishop Felix Davidek

DR. FELIX MARIA DAVÍDEK WAS SMALL IN STATURE, slim, but huge in spirit. He was born in 1921 and died in 1988—a genius sui generis. He was a thinker, a priest and theologian, an activist, a friend, a prisoner, a hero, and later in life, a Roman Catholic bishop. In my judgment, he was first of all a poet. In 1970 Felix was a bishop accepted and fully recognized by Pope Paul VI.

In March, 1970, I was visiting Czechoslovakia. Ludmila Javorová arranged for me to meet Felix under a cloudy night sky in a plowed field between Chrlice and Tuřany. I told Felix why and how I got married. As a bishop, he accepted me into his general jurisdiction behind the Iron Curtain.

Felix encouraged me not to be afraid to secretly celebrate Holy Mass—secretly so as not to disturb and scandalize good Catholics, mostly clergy living in free countries where there was no church persecution. They would not understand; they would not believe.

He instructed me to report his decision concerning my priestly, not clerical, situation to Rome after I left the communist territory, which I did. I received a carefully formulated approval from Rome. To make sure that I understood the message from Rome correctly, I wrote to

Rome again. I received an answer from Bishop Hnilica, the right hand man of Pope Paul VI in the underground church affairs behind the Iron Curtain. The wording was a bit different, but the message was the same. An instruction was added to it: "Do not write to the Vatican again. If you feel you must write, then write to Milano." It also said that the Italian postal services in the hands of the Communist Workers Union had some control over Church correspondence sent to the Vatican. "Do not ask further questions," it concluded.

I realized that I was respected and trusted in spite of my marriage to a Protestant woman. Under Pope Paul VI, the Christian moral theology of love as taught by the German theologian Bernhard Haering, was prevailing even in Rome over the legalistically oriented theology. It was left up to me to exercise with discretion my sacramental Eucharistic priesthood. I have done so for many years.

The same dark night toward morning, Felix and I parted company. He, a man who had suffered so much physical and mental abuse during his fourteen years of imprisonment, had tears in his eyes. Very few people ever saw him tearful.

Felix didn't find any serious theological or psychological grounds against priestly ordination of women in the Roman Catholic Church, except traditional, social, historical and cultural grounds rooted in the tradition of patriarchy and prejudice. After 1970, he ordained five willing women to the priesthood and another five to deaconesses. That became his greatest and unforgivable sin in the eyes of the Roman Curia and other legalistically oriented clergy. Pope John Paul II found it offensive and took a firm stand against it. So did Cardinal Ratzinger, the Pope's right hand man in dogmatic and moral theology teachings. Administratively, it was wise in the context of the current developmental stage of the Church.

There is an interesting, well-written article about Felix in a publication of the *Karlova Universita* published in Prague, Czech Republic, in 2007 (4). Some people consider Felix a saint, while others view him as the devil incarnate. Officially, within the Church administrative structures, he is considered a mentally ill man. Ludmila Javorová, his former Vicar General, told me privately that Felix admitted that he was ill and sometimes not in control of his emotions, particularly after police interrogations. She explained that when Felix was in this state of mind, he would not deal with important matters until he felt better.

Except for possibly Ludmila Javorová, all of the reverend women abdicated their sacramental ordination as invalid under the threat of excommunication, although for years under the communist regime, they secretly celebrated masses, heard confessions, baptized and performed other priestly functions.

Excommunication presupposes a mortal sin, which is a free and malicious intention in a serious moral matter.

Traditionally, a mortal sin meant condemnation to hell. Until recent times, that was the interpretation of excommunication. Today some clergy try to water down the concept of excommunication as if it were exclusion from a club or a brotherhood for not observing club rules. The reverend women understood excommunication in the old traditional way. No wonder they officially abdicated their sacramental ordination after 1990. Who wants to go to hell? There is enough hell already in this world.

48. Patriarchy and Historical Time

IN NATURE, AS IN ORGANIZED HUMAN SOCIETY, WE observe two systems of government. One system is masculine, which is patriarchal, and the other system is feminine or matriarchal.

In the patriarchal system, it is the male who is at the centre of power. His god is male, a father to everybody and everything, even in the hierarchy of minor gods. Judeo-Christian religion is traditionally patriarchal. A patriarch keeps women under his thumb, subservient to him as evidenced in Muslim societies.

In the matriarchal system, the opposite is true. The divinity is feminine. The god is a goddess who controls power and makes all crucial decisions—economic, political and religious. Her style is self-assertive, her power-control subtler yet definite, less prone to using a sword than in the patriarchal approach to governing and expanding territory of control. However, a matriarch may be as cruel as the patriarch when it comes to subordinates.

Western society throughout history has been mainly patriarchal. Since World War II, the Western world seems to be undergoing significant changes. One may observe a gradual, but steady shift, from patriarchy to matriarchy. This shift is becoming more obvious. Educated women have proven again and again that intellectually, scientifically, economically and politically they are equal to males of similar education and talent. Patriarchy is under threat. It is not able to stop this ongoing shift other than by masculine, insensitive, brute force.

It is my understanding that the Catholic Church is not supposed to be patriarchal nor matriarchal. In the name of the mystery of God who is neither male nor female, but a living, creating Love, the Church must keep striving to be a community, a family. That is easier to accomplish on the local levels, like on a parochial level, than on a universal level. In normal, healthy families, the roles of father and mother are complementary and equal in power. That presupposes deep mutual respect between the two sexes. Unfortunately, there is something unhealthy, outdated and even un-Christian in our traditional patriarchal administrative Church system. It is a wonder, almost a miracle that our patriarchal Church functions as well as it does.

Since World War II, the maturing developmental process that I am trying to describe has become more obvious. Vatican II was a milestone. The policies of our recent popes have contributed to this ongoing development. Bishop Felix felt intuitively what was taking place under the surface of the external, visible reality and did something about it by approving ordination of women to the priesthood. The argument of some conservative women that they are women and never felt they had a priestly vocation is shallow. How many men feel they are being called to the priesthood? The great saint Therese of Lisieux always desired to be a priest, but couldn't because she was a woman. She is not the only one.

So much for Felix's thinking and acting.

The second narrative deals with historic time.

In 1958, we students of theology at the Nepomucenum College of Rome were ordered to attend an afternoon lecture at the Lateran Atheneum. The Aula Magna (the large lecture hall) was packed. Professors and a few cardinals were seated in the front row. The two-hour lecture dealt with the recent history of the Church. It was promoted by Pope Pius XII himself.

The lecturer was introduced as an ordinary Italian priest. He was an intellectual, a historian corresponding with significant artists, poets and writers. When we learned of his career as a priest, many of us were shocked. For twenty years he had been excommunicated from the Church as a modernist heretic. It was only his personal friendship with Pope Pius XII that brought him back to the Roman Catholic fold.

After accepting him back into the Church, the pope offered him a high position in the Vatican as head of the Vatican library that contains many precious historical documents. Only historical researchers of high reputation have access to this library, but not without special permission. Our priest lecturer declined that position by telling the pope that he would be quite happy functioning as an ordinary priest serving old and sick people. The pope then asked him to lecture on history at the ecclesiastical universities in Rome. He declined again, but consented to present two lectures: one at the Gregorian University and the other at the Lateran Atheneum. I attended the one at the Lateran.

Out of several seemingly challenging and courageous statements, I vividly remember one on the concept of historical time. It was a revelation for me because it explained the internal dynamism and unavoidable tensions within the Church in the ecumenical sense. The following is a brief summary.

We have chronological measurable time consisting of milliseconds, seconds, hours, days and weeks. It is based on the material dimension of reality of which we are a part. With that time, we become oriented about our past, present and future. The present time is philosophically problematic. The second form of time is psychological time. When have a good, pleasurable time, an hour is experienced as ten minutes. When I am in pain and in depression, ten minutes are experienced as an hour or longer. Psychological time is subjective. It speeds up or slows down according to my feelings. Finally, we have historical time, of which very few people are aware. Most people are not interested in these kinds of observations and explanations.

Historical time spans about sixty years according to the lecturer. At the present year and day, the majority of people are living mentally, emotionally and even culturally forty or more years behind the present; however, there are also some people who are mentally living twenty, thirty or more years ahead of the present time. Most of them are artists, poets, mystics or prophets. They are pioneers leading humanity into the unknown future, pioneers exploring new territory. They are the true leaders, but not formal official leaders. These leaders in the unknown spiritual and invisible territory sometimes commit mistakes. For that they need to be forgiven. Their discoveries and clarifications are often connected with pain—pain of misunderstanding and rejection.

Then the lecturer presented a metaphor. Imagine straight railroad tracks leading far into the horizon. A sixty-car passenger train is moving along the tracks. Each car represents ten years of chronological time. The engine of the train is not in front of the train as most of us imagine it would be, but slightly behind the middle of the train. It pulls and pushes at the same time. The first train cars are almost empty. They are occupied by a few mystics, poets, artists ... the prophets. The cars behind the first car are similar to the first one. They are sparsely occupied by lesser poets and artists. The next car has more people because there are researchers among the lesser poets and artists, university professors and scientists. As we move through the train cars one after the other, we find each one occupied by more people than the previous car. The main function of the engine is co-ordination, holding the train together. The engine operation (the government operation) is rooted in the past with limited foresight of the future because its laws and decisions are based on the well tested experiences of the past and often on problems and circumstances that no longer exist. However, without the engine, the train cannot function as a train moving forward. Without the engine there would be no train, only anarchy. At the end of the train, the cars are overcrowded with people living thirty or forty years in the past.

The passengers who see the engine ahead of them are convinced that the engine leads the train. Anything that interferes with their view is perceived as hostile and destructive, and must be attacked, rejected and destroyed if possible. However, the past cannot return. There is only forward movement. The train is moving faster and faster. These days it is moving at high speed. The people in the first car and in the last car belong to the same train; they are part of the whole.

The Church is a living organism. I believe it is the mystical body of Christ, the body of God incarnated in humanity. The whole history of humanity since its beginning and through all its developmental stages, from bacteria throughout thousands and thousands of years, is a divine creative process. The Church is not an interesting

JIŘÍ (GEORGE) HOŘÁK

museum of comfort and beauty. It is a living organism full of beauty, but also full of painful labour and failures.

Christ is humanity condensed in the person of Jesus Christ, humanity hanging on the cross of history, ridiculed, spat upon, flagellated, crowned with thorns, and loving to the very end. The heart of humanity was pierced to make absolutely sure that "God is dead."

God is not dead! He/She accepted humanity back in His/Her incarnated son. Humanity with its limitations was led astray by the pre-existing, living, spiritual evil symbolized in the form of a knowledgeable but lying serpent, according to the biblical story of Adam and Eve. Humanity was promised by the serpent to become divine, to be God-like.

Humanity on the cross in the representative person of Jesus is ridiculed by whom? Are there other beings in the universe, spiritual beings good and bad, envious of man? Are there invisible, personal forces that are above material dimensions of reality? Science based on material measurements, repeatable experiments and calculations, cannot know. However, we can believe that there are such beings—good ones, corrupt ones—or we can believe that these beings do not exist. Our beliefs do not change anything about their existence or non-existence. Our beliefs, positive or negative, only change our personal and social attitudes and behaviour.

I believe in resurrection, in the victory of love, and in the victory of dignity, even in extreme humiliation and rejection. I believe in the Church, the sacramental Body of Christ, in spite of all its struggles and shortcomings. Its formal institutional beginnings culminate in the manifestation of the person of Jesus of Nazareth. It has been developing throughout centuries by Christ followers to this very day.

My faith in the fact of resurrection, of the final victory of Jesus Christ, makes sense on the background of the universe as we know it today—a universe opened to all kinds of possibilities of life forms. My experience of faith is beyond the realm of science. It can be studied only in psychology with the help of theology. In theology we can study only what people believe and teach about God based on revelations, observations and traditions. We cannot study God himself.

My faith is the same as Bishop Felix's faith. Although we differed and collided on several occasions, we cared about each other.

49. Visit to Czechoslovakia

When I was ordained a priest, my parents were happy. As a boy I often saw my mother on her knees praying. I heard her saying on several occasions: "The floor of hell is paved with the skulls of priests." Where she learned that saying I do not know. She would never miss Holy Mass on Sundays or feast days; neither would my father. My parents' faith was simple, strong and deep.

In 1970, her son the priest married. Now her son's skull would be one of the skulls paving hell. Her high blood pressure increased. She had to be hospitalized. She died at night of a massive stroke because a nurse administered medication without consulting a doctor. This information came from a patient who was with my mother in the same room. My mother was sixty-six years old. When I went to her funeral, my sister Ann showed me beds that my mom had bought for Vera and me for when we visited her in Czechoslovakia.

In was March, 1970, and I didn't know what was happening to me. For no reason I became upset and could not be still. I took Vera's car and drove the whole day along Lake Huron until I was exhausted. When I came home in the evening, Vera told me there was a phone call from Czechoslovakia. Of course she could not understand anything in Czech, but she gave me the number of the caller. It was my brother Tony who reported that my mother had died. He wanted to know whether I would be coming for the funeral. I had no answer, but I promised to phone him back the next day.

For twenty years I couldn't return home without the real danger of being arrested and put in jail. Now I was asked by my brother to take the risk and return for the funeral. I phoned the Czechoslovak Consulate in Montreal and asked whether I could get a visitor's visa with my Canadian passport. They promised to phone me back the next day. My visa was granted.

Vera and I had no money for the trip. I went to the Bank of Montreal on Yonge Street in downtown Toronto and asked for $800.00. The round trip from Toronto to Prague and Ostrava was about $200.00. The currency exchange rate for the Czechoslovak crown was excellent. At the bank I was referred to the manager who gave me, an unemployed old student, the money I requested on the basis of my wife's job. Strange ... nothing was signed. He trusted me and was generous.

The next day I flew to Montreal and then to Prague. I was surprised at the great treatment I received at the airport. An official sitting at the passport window welcomed me and wished me an enjoyable visit after being away so many years. Another man took my unopened luggage and asked me to follow him, explaining that I need not go through all the hassle of being searched like the other passengers. He took me straight to the next plane flying to Ostrava. I felt uncomfortable. Something fishy was in the air.

Tony and my two sisters were waiting for me when I arrived at the Ostrava airport. We drove in Tony's car to the Poruba suburb where my mother had her apartment. In the car they signaled not to talk because the car was probably bugged. This extreme caution on their part continued during my two week visit. My brother Joe was particularly secretive because of his jail term and his past experience in the underground church. During the following two weeks I kept extremely busy visiting and learning about my friends' covert activities on behalf of the Catholic Church headed by Bishop Dr. Felix Maria Davídek.

At the end of my visit, Ann accompanied me to the airport in Prague. There I had to take a Czechoslovak Airlines plane to London where I would fly with British Airlines back to Toronto. I was very tired, yet alert and nervous, anxious about what might happen before I was safely on British soil.

The Czechoslovak airplane destined for London was parked close to the departure hall. About sixty passengers walked in a line to the steps of the plane. Somehow it happened that I was the last one in the line. As I started to walk with the other passengers, two high ranking uniformed police officers joined me. In a friendly manner they enquired about the Czech immigrants in Toronto.

When I reached the steps of the plane, they shook my hand, bowed and gave me a military salute.

Once I was on the plane, I wondered what it was all about. I did not understand it. Several years later these events were clarified and I understood what had happened at the airport.

JIŘÍ (GEORGE) HOŘÁK

VII. YOU ARE PRIEST FOREVER

50. Priest Forever

"TU ES SACERDOS IN AETERNUM SECUNDUM ordinem Melchizedek" are the Latin words the bishop pronounces when he ordains a candidate for priesthood. Translated into English, the statement reads: "You are a priest forever according to the order of Melchizedek."

There is no such a thing as an ex-priest in the Church, despite what many faithful are led to believe. My statement contradicts what the old Roman Catholic Canon Law codex stated: "Sacerdos qui non est clericus in Ecclesia non datur." In English: "A priest that is not a cleric does not exist in the Church." This legal statement is practical, but inconsistent. The fact is, a sacramentally ordained priest is a priest forever. The sacramental order is above the legal, changeable order. A priest may be suspended from his clerical status (that is from his legal employment status), but never from his priestly sacramental status. No longer is he a cleric; therefore he is prohibited from functioning as a priest in Roman Catholic Church.

I am not an ex-priest or a Judas as was implied in quite a few sermons that I heard from the pulpits of some conservative zealous preachers, creating confusion in the minds of the laity. I am an ex-cleric. This fact I accepted without protest. If legal clerical status would be returned to me by a bishop, I could function as a priest again without being re-ordained.

The large administrative structure of the Roman Catholic Church cannot operate without laws and regulations. Without them there would be inconsistencies and various doctrines similar to the Protestant denominations.

On one occasion, a congregation of the faithful was gathered for a Sunday mass in the church, but no priest was available. I could have filled in, but I didn't, because I didn't want to upset anybody. To my knowledge, the Anglican Church is more progressive in dealing with such situations with their "ex-priests."

I am not saying anything new; I'm only trying to clarify for reflecting Catholic laity where our modern problems lie. I am not rebellious and certainly not a revolutionary. I see Christian life with its struggles from the large perspective based on my Catholic, updated life experience.

Recently I went to my barber shop for a haircut. There were four women cutting hair for men and women. One of the four addressed me with a question: "Were you a priest?"

I wasn't too surprised by this because I had heard this kind of embarrassing question before.

"Yes," I replied. "What makes you think so?"

"You look like one," she said as she gave me a hug and a kiss. No Roman collar, no badge, nothing clerical that could indicate my priesthood. In the conversation that followed, she told me she was a Protestant.

When I got my first job at the Crippled Children's summer camp in 1969, I was emptying garbage cans into the pickup truck, dressed in shorts and a t-shirt. I stopped for a chat with five university students standing in a semi-circle. A curious twelve-year-old First Nations youth joined the group. After a few minutes and without any hesitation, he pointed his finger at me and said, "You are a priest."

I was surprised, but calmly asked why he'd said that.

"You are a priest," he repeated. "I know it." As we had just met and I was not wearing anything to indicate I was a priest, how could he have known?

One November day during a heavy snowfall, I made a reservation for a private retreat weekend with the Benedictine monks in Georgetown, Ontario. When I walked into the common guest room on Friday evening, I found some men having coffee with the monk in charge of the guests. He welcomed me with a surprised voice in front of everybody, "Why didn't you tell me on the phone that you are a priest?"

Something similar happened later in another monastery where I brought a group of men for a weekend retreat. They didn't know my priestly background, but when we walked into the guest area of the monastery, the monk in charge said to me in front of the group, "Why didn't you tell me that you are a priest? We would have prepared a special room for you." My group of men didn't know anything about my background.

After a Cursillo (a kind of a religious retreat), a large group of participants met monthly for Ultreas (Spanish name for follow up meetings). There were about thirty of us, men and women. Everybody in the group knew Vera as my wife and their joke master. At the end of one of our Ultreas, the leader of the evening announced, "Now, George will give us all his blessing!" I was annoyed, but I complied. When everybody left, I asked the leader why he picked me. I said that I didn't want to publicize my priestly background among Roman Catholics so as not to confuse them. He apologized and explained that he had asked for my blessing spontaneously; he didn't know that I was an ordained priest.

When Vera and I were living in Mississauga, we socialized with a common law couple who had many problems and yet, in spite of much mutual abuse, had stayed together. He was a Catholic and quite intelligent and sensitive, but he was also an aggressive drunkard. One day when they came for a visit he announced, "George, last night I had a dream about you. I saw you dressed in long white robe, standing at the altar."

Currently I am living in a retirement home. Most of the residents are Protestants. There are over one hundred residents here and quite a few staff taking care of us. Some are non-believers and agnostics. Somehow the word spread that I am a retired priest. I am treated politely and respectfully by everybody. There are no signs of prejudice and hostility from anybody.

I close this story with an observation that is superficial from a psychological point of view, but realistic, humorous and sad from the pragmatic point of view. There are two opposite extremes in the general population of humanity. Between those two extremes there exists a gradation of characters from one extreme to the other. In the upper extreme are people with great sensitivity and intuitiveness. In the lower extreme are people with heads that you could chop wood on and nothing would change. They are stable, reliable and immovable in their convictions. It doesn't make any difference whether they are Catholics, Protestants or atheists.

This is not a religious matter. It is a psychological problem. Such people consider themselves and are considered by their followers as strong and virtuous. Unfortunately, with their convictions they are often insensitive and cruel, incapable of deeper, true love.

Stubbornness is not necessarily faithfulness. Faithfulness and respect of one's sacramental priesthood is a privilege to be treasured to the very end of earthly life. I am grateful for it all.

JIŘÍ (GEORGE) HOŘÁK

51. York University

I ACCUMULATED EIGHT UNDERGRADUATE CREDITS, mostly in psychology, and then I quit. From those eight courses I will mention only two that might be of interest. I took Introduction to Sociology at Atkinson College, an affiliate of York University. There was no oral examination. The evaluation consisted of a ten-page autobiographical paper. My paper was returned to me by the assistant to the professor with a B mark and a half page comment written in red. It stated that my life story was a fabrication.

I went to see the assistant to explain that what I had written was true and asked him how he arrived at his conclusion. His explanation was simple. He said that if what I had written were true, I would never have been able to become a university student. My objections were useless. The B mark remained. In his eyes my writing was creative writing.

The other course that I really enjoyed for its dynamism was Psychology of Religion. It was taught by Professor David Bakan, a Freudian in a psychology faculty oriented toward behaviourism. Of those two orientations in psychology, I preferred the Freudian one, although I am not a Freudian. I liked Professor Bakan for his authenticity, his gentleness and also his arrogant, transparent manner. You knew where you stood with him; you could be candid with him and he would not be offended.

Psychologically speaking, his religious insights were quite interesting. Occasionally he would muse in a quiet voice that was still audible if you were sitting close to him in a classroom of about thirty students. He would say to himself, "It is possible that Jesus of Nazareth was the Messiah." And then he would reply, "No, that cannot be!"

His religious views were interesting. He said openly in class that he had no use for Protestantism, but he respected Roman Catholics. He admired Roman Catholics' psychological shrewdness, knowing how to keep emotions going. "You come to a Roman Catholic church," he said, "and what do you see? There is a big cross with a man who was tortured, nailed to the cross and killed. The emotions of disgust and anger start to emerge in you. Then you turn around and what do you see? There is a young beautiful lady with a child at her breast. Tender loving emotions start to emerge in you, and suddenly you realize that the little baby in her arms is the man on the cross. Who committed such a terrible crime? Who crucified that beautiful baby? Jews! Who else but Jews? Let's get the Jews!"

When the course on Psychology of Religion was over, we received our marks. My mark was a minimal pass. I was surprised, so I went to see Professor Bakan to find out why it was so low.

"Because you did not submit your paper," he explained.

"I did submit my paper," I said, "and I was one of the first ones who did."

He shoved a pile of papers in front of me. "Show me your paper."

Indeed, my paper was not there. As I went through the papers, I realized that some papers had been written for a class other than Psychology of Religion. Those papers had inconsistent content. The words religion and psychology were sneaked into them here and there by the writers—obviously poor and transparent cheating, but in Bakan's eyes they had done a better job than I had. I started to wonder whether the professor had actually read the papers.

The situation between us became confrontational.

"Ha, a classic Freudian slip," I said. "You didn't like my paper, so you lost it."

"Prove to me that you wrote the paper," he demanded.

"I can do that. It is a one-hour drive to my home where I have a copy. I can be back in two hours. Obviously in two hours I cannot write a paper. Will you be here when I come back in two hours?"

He consented, and I was back with a copy of my paper in two hours. He looked at it, but he didn't open it. He threw it in the garbage can stammering, "What do you want from me?"

"A+," I said.

"Here is your A, now go."

I smiled and left. I knew the real problem: the paper was about Satan.

In my ignorance, I thought it would be easy to write a paper on Satan. After all, we had read about the existence of evil spirits in the Bible. Christ was exorcising them; Catholics have protective exorcising prayers. Witches practice exorcisms; in the Ignatian exercises we have a section strictly concerned with the discernment of spirits.

When I started to write the paper in a more scientific fashion, I soon realized that I had chosen a difficult topic. I contacted a professor of the Old Testament to enlighten me. He explained that in antiquity, the name Satan was the name in the Middle East for the Lord of the Flies. Therefore, under the same name we have two different realities. In the Christian tradition the name Satan does not mean the Lord of the Flies, from where the name originated, but refers to a spiritual being much more intelligent and powerful than the Lord of the Flies. It means the shrewd lord of evil spirits.

Before addressing the psychology of religion, I need to talk about religion itself, a subject of many studies and unpleasant arguments—an unpopular and confusing subject. To talk about religion means to talk about faith. To talk about faith in a strictly analytical way is difficult. Students, and often their professors, lack the necessary deep and subtle sacred experiences and intuitive insights that come to us in focused prayers and devotional practices.

JIŘÍ (GEORGE) HOŘÁK

Poetry, art, parables, solitude, prayer, silence, meditation, self-discipline and nature's beauty are some of the
tools that lead to insights and convictions that are deeper
than the convictions of reality-limiting rationalism
edging sometimes on the irrational and culminating in an
easy-going pragmatism. Rationalism is a closed system of
thinking different from being rational and open-minded.

The fact that Professor Bakan threw my paper on Satan
in the garbage in my presence without even looking at it,
put a smile on my face. Obviously he had seen it before.
In awarding me an A grade, he revealed not only his
disgust, but also his honesty. Clearly he refused to take
seriously what I had written. I never stopped liking him.
There was nothing phony about the professor.

52. Probation and Parole

VERA KEPT WORKING AND I ATTENDED YORK University to accumulate the undergraduate credits necessary for admission to graduate studies in clinical psychology. From time to time Vera and I visited Madonna House in Combermere for two days and a night. Everything was working the way we planned it, but I didn't feel very good about our situation. In my upbringing, it was the male who was supposed to support his wife, not the other way around.

I was no longer in my twenties. How long would it take before I graduated with a PhD in Clinical Psychology, if I managed to graduate at all? That was the question in the back of my mind. Also, I experienced some difficulties in coping with the young university students. In the cafeteria they saw me as a professor rather than as one of them.

During one of our visits to Madonna House, I met an Irish fellow. During our friendly chat, I told him about my background and my present situation as a student. He made me an offer. He said that he was a friend of Mr. McLaughlin who was the head of the Probation and Parole Department in the Attorney General of Ontario's office. Probation and parole was a relatively new government department and still in the developmental stages, although it was already functioning well.

Mr. McLaughlin was looking for men like me, namely priests and Protestant ministers, because they proved to be among his best officers. I did

n't know anything about probation and parole, but I liked the idea of a new challenge, and also the fact that it was steady and reliable employment. I decided to give it a try. Through my Irish friend, I met with Mr. McLaughlin. After a friendly interview which included a discussion about Catholics, Anglicans and Protestants, he hired me.

I started my first assignment in Brampton, Ontario in November of 1971. I quit my university studies, eager to learn about probation, parole and the federal and provincial criminal justice systems. Vera and I moved to Brampton into a large two-bedroom apartment. It was easy for Vera to commute by train to downtown Toronto. Our income increased significantly.

There were three probation and parole officers in Brampton, two men and one woman, assisted by two secretaries. I replaced the woman officer who had been promoted to a higher position in the Ontario government.

My training consisted of spending many hours as an observer at the Provincial Criminal Court, Juvenile Court and County Court. In the evenings when everybody went home, I was in the office studying individual probation and parole files and learning about the three aspects of probation: administration, criminal law and social work.

My two colleagues helped me immensely. Bob was a former police officer and Alf a former Presbyterian minister. Soon I got to know the court employees, some of the lawyers, judges and several police departments in the Brampton area of Peel County. The unified Peel Regional Police did not yet exist.

I started to feel comfortable belonging to the sophisticated criminal justice system. I became involved, particularly with the social work dimension of probation and parole. I soon realized that not all officers in the province shared my orientation. The easiest way to perform a probation and parole officer's tasks without sweating too much was to focus on the administrative aspects of the job, not on individual people. That approach was not my cup of tea. I worked many overtime hours in the social dimension of my new job, just as Vera did as a social worker. We could afford it. Both of us were healthy and we had no children. Vera worked mostly with single mothers and their children. Our marriage was working wonderfully. Mentally and spiritually, we were moving in the same direction.

I could tell many stories about my experiences with "criminals" and their families, or lack of families ... stories about criminal courts, jails, schools, lawyers and police. I dealt not only with criminals, but with all kinds of attitudes within the hierarchically structured, administrative government system. Three probation cases will provide a sample of my work.

My first serious case in Brampton was a fellow assigned to me with a warning that he was a dangerous man. He was about thirty years old and living on a farm in the Brampton area. He was angry and aggressive. People were afraid of him, particularly our two secretaries. He wouldn't listen to what I had to tell him and kept asking me who I thought I was. My previous clinical pastoral training in a psychiatric hospital came in handy. I knew that behind his aggressive attitude was a deep-seated fear and unhappiness. He warned me that a loaded rifle hung near the entrance to his house, and if I ever dared to come to his farm, it would be the end of me. My response was that the rifle was fine with me and that he should expect my visit later that afternoon.

Later in the afternoon, I found his house and knocked on the door. Everything was locked, and there was no response to my knocking and bell ringing. But there was a welcoming greeter in the yard—a big St. Bernard dog. When he saw me, he walked toward me, got up on his back legs, and put his paws on my shoulders so that he almost knocked me over; our noses almost touched and our eyes briefly met. I told him that I liked him. It was true.

After several months, this threatening, dangerous "criminal" cried like a baby in my office; I had to play the role of an accepting, loving mother. He told me how he "beat the shit" out of his cruel old man as soon as he was old enough and strong enough. He got in touch with his repressed guilt feelings deeply buried under his external rough, aggressive behaviour.

On another case, I received an order from the court for pre-sentence reports on three teenagers who were convicted of breaking into houses and stealing TVs and electronic equipment. After their convictions, all three were temporally incarcerated before sentencing. In preparing the reports on them, I had to check on their family background, their education, social environment and attitudes. It was obvious to me that the oldest boy was the organizer and leader.

When I interviewed him at the old Brampton jail, I found a tall, healthy, handsome, blond young man who was calm, self-confident and arrogant. He laughed at me, ridiculing my work as useless comedy. In his view, the result of it all would be the same—just another insignificant probation order, similar to several in the past. It took me almost an hour before we started to talk seriously. I told him that it was gutless for him to use two naive teenagers to steal for him. Not only that, I told him that he was not the real leader because what they stole had to be sold in order to get money. The "salesman" was the real leader who was using him so he was no smarter than his two younger accomplices.

"Who is the real leader?" I asked. He refused to tell me.

I mentioned that I was going to see his parents that evening. He said that he couldn't care less about them. His parents were rich and didn't care about him. They always provided him with an expensive criminal lawyer, not because they loved him, but because he was an embarrassment to them. "You'll see tonight how nice they'll treat you," he said. I promised him that I would do my best to get him locked behind bars for two years. I also told him my report might influence the sentencing judge. He laughed and said we would see about that.

That evening I went to meet his parents. I was welcomed into their large, comfortable home. Both parents were well dressed and friendly. The fireplace was burning. They rolled a liquor cabinet into the living room, asking me what I preferred. They apologized for their son. My interview with them was co-operative and pleasant. I realized that their son was telling the truth about being an embarrassment to his parents.

In the pre-sentence section of the report on the circumstances surrounding the commission of the crime, I presented the true picture of the case as I perceived it: namely that the two younger followers were involved with the older leader, but also that the main culprit, the "salesman" and instigator of the criminal activities, was not mentioned in the police report. He was not found, and he was not charged. The judge appreciated this information, but the Crown Attorney and the police did not.

My friend was sentenced to eighteen months in jail. The day after the sentencing I had another interview at the Brampton jail. When I spoke to the guard at the door, my new friend recognized my voice and shouted from behind the bars, "Mr. Horak! Mr. Horak, come here! I want to talk to you." I cautiously approached the bars, staying a safe distance from the prisoner. There was no such danger in this case. My imprisoned friend introduced me to the other prisoners, telling them proudly that I was his probation officer, a friend, someone who finally took him seriously. "To hell with my parents," he said. "I'll go on my own. I'll study while I'm serving my sentence and finish high school."

I have no idea whether he followed through with his plan, what happened to him while serving his six-month sentence or where he is today. Six of the eighteen months were forgiven for good behaviour. He served another six months in a halfway house in the community. An eighteen month jail sentence meant only six months in jail.

After several years, I was settled and comfortable with my probation work. When I had a breach of probation case in Brampton or Mississauga or Toronto, often I had to wait for a long time in the courthouse before the case was called. Out of curiosity, I would walk into the courtrooms to observe the proceedings. I found most of the trials boring, but from time to time there was an interesting case, like the following incident that took place in the Mississauga provincial courthouse.

As I opened the door to one of the courtrooms, I was stopped by a uniformed police officer who told me to stay out. I knew the judge who was presiding over a preliminary hearing on a murder case, deciding whether there was enough evidence to proceed before judge and jury. As the police officer was pushing me out the door, the judge spotted me. He instructed the officer to allow me in. The courtroom was empty except for the accused and the arguing parties, a famous criminal defense lawyer and the Crown Attorney. I observed the proceedings. After about twenty minutes, the judge stopped the proceedings for ten minutes and invited me to his chamber.

Judge Old was upset, pacing and back and forth. "George," he said. "I don't know what to do. What should I do? It's against my conscience, but I have to let the murderer go. I haven't the slightest doubt that I have the murderer in front of me, but his defense lawyer is excellent on technicalities and the Crown Attorney is unable to measure up to him."

What really happened was simple. The accused had gone to Florida on vacation, leaving his wife at home alone. When he returned, he found his murdered wife and called police. At that time, according to Judge Old, a professional murder in Toronto would cost $10,000. Few people could afford an expensive professional murder service and a first class defense lawyer.

When I was first learning about probation and parole work, my Brampton instructors included a paragraph in the pre-sentence report under the heading "Circumstances Surrounding the Commission of the Offence." Sometimes this paragraph became problematic for the Crown Attorney, particularly when the defense attorney negotiated in the Crown Attorney's office to proceed under lesser charges than the original charges laid by the police. Occasionally it created a situation in which the judge, after reading that paragraph, got a different picture of the criminal offence than what was presented to him by the Crown Attorney in the courtroom. In some instances, it placed the Crown Attorney and the police in an awkward or even embarrassing situation in which they had to explain to the judge what really happened and why the Crown was proceeding in one way and not in another.

In my initial zeal, I took the Circumstances paragraph seriously. That landed me in hot water. The chief Crown Attorney in Brampton, an older man, came to our probation office to have a word with me. Then he approached my supervisor to complain that I was doing investigations, which was not my business—it was police business. The new information concerning the offence always came from my interview with the offender, an interview that was frequently in the form of a friendly, straightforward chat.

There was some re-organization taking place in the Ontario government at that time; our department of Probation and Parole was moved to the Ministry of Correctional Services. My local troubles with the Circumstances paragraph in my pre-sentence reports ended at our Toronto head office. I was called there and admonished to stop "rocking the boat." I considered my situation dangerous employment-wise and complained to the senior judge in Brampton, Judge August. He got angry in a polite way and ordered our new head of Probation and Parole and his assistant in Toronto to meet with him.

Obviously he lectured them in my absence ... the body language of both men conveyed that fact as they left the judge's office. They were not hostile towards me, but rather respectful. The decision was to remove the Circumstances paragraph from the pre-sentence reports. No more "investigation" on the part of a probation officer. It never was my intention to conduct a police investigation. It just happened.

53. Staff Training Officer

AFTER FIVE YEARS IN THE PROBATION AND PAROLE field, I felt content with my accomplishments and the many friends I had made. One day Chuck Stewart, a criminologist, approached me and described the ongoing upgrading of the staff training department, now within the Ministry of Correctional Services. He said that the restructuring of the staff training department was a challenging and creative venture, and that he and his colleagues were looking for people like me. All I had to do was submit my resume with an application for one of three new staff training officer positions. If I were accepted on the basis of my submission, I would be called for an interview. The new position would move me from the union bargaining unit into the management unit of the Ontario civil service. I submitted my application as Chuck suggested and soon after was called for an interview.

The interview, which was strange and tough, was conducted by Chuck and two others. They didn't sit behind a desk ask questions and thoughtfully consider the answers. Instead, they sat apart without a desk in a large room asking one question after another. They interrupted during my answers, cutting each other off in mid-sentence. The more they barked at me, the more I felt alert and angry, while externally keeping my composure. The interview lasted over an hour. Two weeks later I received notification that I had been successful in the competition.

I was told there were three positions open: one in Guelph for western Ontario, one in Brampton for central Ontario, and one in Cobourg for the eastern Ontario. As number one on the list of successful candidates, I was allowed to choose from the three openings. Naturally, I chose Cobourg, about 160 kilometres east of Toronto, where Chuck became the leader and supervisor.

Later I asked him about the unusual interview. He responded with a laugh, explaining that it was set up intentionally. The interview method was developed by American army psychologists during the war to select and train army officers in a short time. I took that explanation as a compliment. Chuck also told me that some of the applicants were much better qualified than I was, but they had quit during the interview.

There were four officers and two secretaries in the Cobourg staff training department: Chuck; John, who came from the old staff training department; Bill, an impressive Irish fellow who had been a Baptist minister and later a Presbyterian minister, and me. When Bill and I met and I told him that I was a Jesuit, he exploded with disgust.

"What? The worst people under the sun," he exclaimed.

I laughed at Bill's spontaneity and sincerity. We had an immediate connection and he became a close friend. Vera and I spent many beautiful weekends with Bill and his wife at their cottage and they visited us in Durham.

In my new position, I was faced with a steep learning curve. Our main customers were correctional officers and guards working in jails and correctional institutions. Some of the older guards had very little training. When they were hired, they were given the keys to a jail with their shift assignment and that was it. Big men and former soldiers were the preferred jail employees. That hiring approach was terminated and the new staff training department was expected to lead the way.

It was not expected, but I requested a prison guard uniform so I could experience what it was like to be a guard. I wanted to know the difficulties and frustrations of the job; I wanted to learn more from personal involvement than from theory. I was provided with the uniform without question. The superintendents of correctional institutions and of jails appreciated my approach. They welcomed me wherever I went, sharing their techniques and frustrations.

Prison guards do not have the best public image. I found that 90 per cent were kind and compassionate people who had to do unpleasant work day after day, and night after night. In a way they were prisoners, locked in, with the only difference being that they could go home at the end of their shift. I moved freely among them in various jails and institutions whenever I could, during their day shifts and also at night. Chuck supported me in my efforts.

In our Staff Training Centre in Cobourg, we regularly ran two week courses for groups of a dozen male and sometimes female correctional officers. My Czech accent was not much of a problem, except that it made me a bit different from the others. Some people asked friendly questions about my background, but others didn't like a "foreigner" among them. This was not the situation in large cities like Toronto where there were many foreign accents and I blended in.

One of the first requirements of the new job was to pass the St. John's Ambulance instructor certification course. The examiner, who seemed to be motivated by my foreign accent, focused on me during the practical tests. He picked me to answer difficult medical emergency problems more frequently than the others. I got the certificate.

The next training exercise was a one-day course in crowd and riot control that took place in Belleville at the Ontario police training facility. There were about thirty police officers in uniforms and two policewomen. I was the only civilian among them. They were polite and respectful towards me, "a foreigner." After a theoretical lecture based on American cities' experiences, we were taken to a large gym under the command of a sergeant. I was issued a helmet and a police baton, the same as everybody else in the group, and we marched around with the two policewomen and me at the end of the formation. Then we practiced defense and attack formations used in riot control.

Later the sergeant put us in a single line facing him. He walked up to me and shouted instructions. I don't remember what he was shouting, but I remember how I felt. His nose was almost touching mine. I felt insulted and angry; I struggled to control myself from hitting him with my baton. I appreciated my Jesuit training in humility and obedience. He knew what he was doing; he was provoking me. He ordered me to stand beside him in the middle of the gym.

"Take over!" he demanded.

I didn't know the police commands, but I started to command anyway. "Turn right!" I ordered, and all the officers did. "March! Left, right, left, right..." The officers started to march. I had a feeling of control and power, but I was uncertain what was coming next. I was impressed with the men and the two women. Obviously they knew what the sergeant was doing and sympathized with me. Good people!

"That's enough," the sergeant said as he took over command. I stepped into the last line of the formation with the two female officers at my sides and silently repeated in my mind, *Left, right, left, right...* Actually, it was the same marching as I had practiced as a youngster in the Orel Gym (Aquila gymnastic organization in

Czechoslovakia) in our town before and after the war. When the day was over, the sergeant was polite to me.

My training with tear gas and other gases took place at the military base near Kingston. The army officers treated me as gentlemen, as if I were one of them. They asked questions about the communist regime in Czechoslovakia.

A one-day course about administration in the federal government took place in Ottawa. There were about twelve students coming from different departments, all gathered around a large conference table. Before the course started, we briefly introduced ourselves. I introduced myself by saying, "My name is George Horak, but my real name in Czech is Jiří Hořák. It became George Horak because people could not pronounce the difficult sound of ř." To my surprise, the man next to me said in good Czech with a smile, "Jiří Hořák." We met at lunch and on several other occasions in Toronto. I learned that he was a lawyer who had been a judge in Czechoslovakia during the years of severe communist oppression. Now he felt embarrassed and guilty about it. He had managed to get out of the communist system and had landed in England. From there he had immigrated with his wife and son to Canada.

During one of our lunch meetings I told him the story of my visit to Czechoslovakia in 1970 for my mother's funeral. It puzzled my suspicious mind why the communist police officers had treated me so well, particularly at the Prague airport when I was leaving the country. I reasoned that because he had been part of the communist system in administration, he might have an explanation.

He did. He told me that the plane was parked close to the departure exit. The wall facing the departing planes was glass. Behind the glass was a photographer who I could not see. He took pictures of me with the two Czech police officers accompanying me to the steps of the plane. The photographer was also recording my conversation with the two police officers who were equipped with hidden microphones. This was the simple explanation of this staged performance.

Some of the best communist spies were not the people sent under false pretences to foreign countries, but people already settled in foreign countries, people who compromised themselves and provided the communist intelligence with information. Obviously that was the motive for the police behaviour and their military salute at the end at the Prague airport.

54. Was it RCMP?

AFTER ABOUT TWO YEARS WORKING IN COBOURG, there was a reorganization of the staff training department. Chuck became superintendent of a jail. My close friend Bill retired. I was transferred to the Brampton Staff Training Office where my supervisor was Dr. Leheurusie, an Englishman who had lived in Africa. We understood each other quite well. From Brampton, I was sent to Guelph to run staff training courses for the western part of the province as far north as Thunder Bay. Vera continued her work at the Toronto Metropolitan Children's Aid Society, commuting by Go-Train from Mississauga.

When I worked in Cobourg, I had a private one-bedroom apartment and drove home to Mississauga on weekends. Occasionally on Friday evenings, Vera came to Cobourg by train, and then on Saturday morning we would drive together back to Mississauga. It was my practice to keep a reserve key for the main entrance to our house in Mississauga hidden in a secret place outside the house. The key was hidden in a small magnetic box attached to the left bottom inside corner of our metallic garage door which was never locked. Vera wasn't concerned about such things and didn't pay attention when I explained to her where and why I hid the extra key.

One winter day late in the afternoon when I returned to my apartment in Cobourg, there was a phone call from Vera. In the morning when left for work, she had forgotten her keys. The door had locked automatically without the key, but without the key it could not be opened. She wanted to know where I had hidden the reserve key. I told her. In a few minutes she phoned back, telling me in an upset voice that somebody had broken into our house. It had never happened before, just on this particular day when she forgot her keys. I instructed her not to move anything in the house and to call the police. I would be home in two hours. She followed my instructions.

A uniformed officer arrived before I returned. He shrugged his shoulders and told Vera that break and enters were a daily occurrence, and because they were so frequent, it was beyond police ability to deal with them. The constables took a sheet of plywood that I had in the basement and nailed it to the basement window through which the "thief" had entered from the back of our house.

By the time I arrived, the police officer had already left without bothering to go through the house. I went through all the rooms and realized that the whole house had been searched. Some drawers were left half-open, but there was no damage. The only damage was to my desk. A locked drawer in which I had personal and banking documents had been forcefully opened, and the money and documents were lying on the floor. Strange! What was the "thief" after if he had not even taken the cash?

A year later, after I was transferred from Cobourg to Brampton, I mentioned the incident to my new boss, Dr. Leherusie. He smiled and explained that it was not done by ordinary thieves or teenagers. It was a well planned and executed professional search either by communist intelligence or RCMP intelligence.[11] "For some reason they are after you," he said. I wondered whether the secret service of the RCMP had talked to him or somebody else behind my back.

What my friend, the former judge had explained to me about the incident at the Prague airport in 1970 and the break and enter that followed several years later, connected in my mind.

It's publicly known that in the intelligence services there are compromised double agents who are working for both sides, for two enemy countries. Since the Czechoslovak intelligence attempt to get me entangled in their net failed, it could be revenge to expose me to the RCMP as a communist agent through the film and the recorded conversation of my encounter with the two uniformed police officers at the Prague airport in 1970. Naturally, I would be a person of interest to the RCMP, probably even considered a sleeping communist intelligence cell. That would certainly be unpleasant for my wife and me. The best defense of my innocence was to smile and ignore it all. Let the RCMP find the truth.

Another interesting revelation occurred a few years after the collapse of communism in Czechoslovakia. The

Czechoslovak government opened secret police files for public inspection. The files compromised people who had secretly co-operated with the communists as spies within the country during the oppressive communist years. I had no interest in those archives until I started to write this memoir. I wanted to see the secret material concerning my friends and me. I asked one of my nephews in Brno to check the archives in my name. What he found and sent to me in the form of photocopies was insignificant, except for one thing. On September 19, 1955, the head of the Ministry of Interior in Gottwaldov, officer Matějka, requested from the branch of the same Ministry in Plzeň, information about my whereabouts and ordered a special file opened on me.

Someone mentioned that the Plzeň branch kept archives about Czechs and Slovaks in foreign countries. When I asked to see this file, I learned that such a file did not exist. Obviously, files of former Czechoslovak citizens living "illegally" (according to the communists) outside of their native country were either destroyed or hidden at the time of the great political changes in Czechoslovakia in the early 1990s before the ordinary police archives were opened to the public. The destroyed files would compromise those who co-operated as spies for the communists outside of the country. Nobody can find out who they were.

All this is now history. It is a sad commentary on humanity and Godless humanistic ideals.

55. The Portrait Painter

SALLY, WHO HAD WORKED FOR VERA'S FAMILY IN
Newfoundland most of her life, arrived at our house on
one of those postcard-perfect Ontario summer days.
Sixty years old, she had never been to Ontario. Vera, a
generous person to the marrow of her bones, wanted to
show Sally the time of her life. Vera prepared the guest
bedroom of our townhouse with care, adding fresh
flowers to give it that "Better Homes and Gardens"
touch. For the next week, Vera was her hostess and I her
trusty assistant.

We visited Toronto city hall, Yonge Street, and the
shopping malls that seemed to go on forever. We toured
the picturesque countryside of the Niagara Peninsula,
the churches, and, of course, Niagara Falls.

One afternoon we drove to the Ontario Place amuse-
ment park located on a manmade island built in Lake
Ontario. We strolled through the rides and craft booths,
taking in the smells of the ethnic foods. Everyone had
something to sell. In the shade of colourful umbrellas sat
four portrait artists. For $5.00 they would sketch your
portrait in black and white; for $10, you could have a
colour portrait.

I have always had an interest in whatever was alive and authentic. Like many other curious people, we stopped and looked over the shoulders of the painters, comparing what we saw on their sketching blocks to the models sitting on chairs in front of them. One of the painters, a man in his forties, bearded with dishevelled hair and looking a bit like a street person, was sketching a black woman. Looking at her and then back at the sketch in progress, I remarked quite spontaneously, "Isn't she beautiful. I can see her when I look at the sketch."

Two people immediately reacted to my words. The artist lifted his head and looked at me, and a big black man on my right gave me a hostile look. I realized that I was speaking about his wife. I silently and calmly apologized to him and he accepted my apology in a similar fashion by mere eye contact. He and his wife were visitors to Toronto from New York City.

After they left, I asked the artist what he was doing among the student painters. He said that he was making a fast buck so that he could eat and have a place to sleep. In the brief discussion that followed, I learned that he was a university fine arts graduate. The early years of his career had been spent painting landscapes, but recently he had discovered people.

He then pointed with his unshaved chin to his three colleagues sketching young women in front of other spectators. "There is nothing there to paint," he said. "What you see are beautiful shapes, empty containers, but not much life. But that black woman was full of life. She has overcome a lot of troubles and sufferings which are written all over her face. She is victorious. To do her justice I would need at least ten hours, not just fifteen minutes. I paint only what I see and nothing else. Look," he reached under his seat and pulled out a colour sketch, "this man threw this angrily on my head a while ago and left without paying." It was a picture of a well dressed businessman with an aggressive, arrogant face. "Without saying so, he wanted me to paint him as somebody he is not. Sit down." He made a quick sketch of me, a little bit of a caricature. On a light blue background, he drew a head that was disproportionately large from the nose up. I paid him for it.

What a gift to be able to see beyond appearances, to appreciate the beauty, growth, stagnation, degeneration, joy and pain of each individual struggle on the human journey. Displayed for all to see, yet how many of us truly see?

56. Witchcraft

WITCHCRAFT IS ALIVE AND WELL IN OUR MODERN society. I experienced witchcraft for the first time at the age of nineteen at Horní Štěpánov. One of Felix's hobbies was anthropology. On a few occasions he sent me to interview people suspected of being witches.

How did our modern society arrive at its highly rationalistic attitude of the twentieth century, denying spiritual realities? Why is part of our educated society turning from the rational back to the irrational, imaginary and wild? To answer these questions one needs to learn about the development of human thought. Like a pendulum, the rational and irrational, one extreme attracts the other.

The European Christian Protestant and Catholic armies in Europe fought for thirty years in the seventeenth century. After thirty years of bloodshed and destruction in the name of their teaching and their faith in Christ, they finally arrived at a compromise and a political settlement—Cuius regio eius religio, which means if the lord of a region was a Protestant, all people in his territory had to be Protestant; if he was a Catholic, then all had to become Catholic.

The religious doctrines at that time were not providing a solution for the political and economic problems. Therefore, some thinkers arrived at the conclusion that the solution would not be found in the level of faith, but in rationality. Everything that cannot be measured, tested by experiments and mathematics, must be excluded, ignored as if it did not exist, because it's not rational. In other words, what was not measurable or visible was assumed to be non-existent.

This strictly rationalistic method became successful on the level of matter and technology. It intentionally ignored spiritual realities, not only religious ones, but also non- religious ones, like witchcraft. Methodical exclusion of something does not stop its existence.

Information concerning witchcraft and paranormal phenomenon online is accessible to everyone, children included. In popular terms, witchcraft is the practice of casting spells and manipulating praeter-natural forces for fun, profit, and harming others.

Dr. Leherusie and I had several discussions that did not seem to interest others. On one occasion, he suggested that I take a short spiritual course. I knew nothing about it, but I went for it.

The centre was an ashram located northeast of Toronto. It was a farm house renovated as a lecture hall and for guest accommodations. In a nearby field, there was a shrine built in an oriental style by two Buddhist monks who had returned to their community after completing their mission in Canada.

The course started on Friday evening and finished on Sunday afternoon. The staff operating the facility were mostly university students. They politely served us in the dining room. Everything seemed fine, yet I felt uncomfortable in the chilly and serious atmosphere. I was curious.

The lectures were given by a woman visiting from England. She gave the impression of a person in charge of the centre, although she was a guest lecturer only. She kept explaining that humankind on this earth is surrounded by different kinds of spirits, many eager to serve as our helpers. It was a teaching parallel to the Church teaching on angels, particularly about guardian angels as I learned in my childhood. The focus of her message on the existence of such spiritual beings, their wisdom and power, was consistent during the entire course.

According to the lecturer, the miracle of Dunkirk, when the English army was surrounded by the German army that could have annihilated it, was the result of all the English witch covens uniting to cast a spell that paralyzed the Germans for nine days. That allowed the English army to return to England. One of my former supervisors, Mr. Beatty, was an officer in that English army trapped at Dunkirk. He described the anxious times they had and their inability to understand why the Germans had not swept them into the sea.

JIŘÍ (GEORGE) HOŘÁK

The lecturer stressed that every one of us has a personal spiritual guide available. All we have to do is call upon him and ask for his name. If he appears to us and gives us his name, he will be ready to help us in difficult life situations.

On Sunday after lunch, I was strolling around the property with a woman who had attended the course to try to find some explanation for her personal paranormal experiences. As we talked, she mentioned that she was a Roman Catholic. She told me she felt guilty because for the first time she had missed Sunday mass. I told her that she didn't have to miss mass if she lived in Toronto because there was a late mass at the cathedral. She also revealed that she had come to this place only because she had approached several priests for help, but none of them knew what she was talking about and could not help her. Now, finally, she was getting answers to her anxious inquiries.

How could priests understand her? Paranormal phenomenon is not taught in the seminaries. It's a matter that belongs not only to psychiatry, but also to the realm of spirituality. Our Catholic theology gradually slipped from being rational to becoming more rationalistic. Rationalism is found in technology and research in the material dimensions of reality, but it's inadequate in spiritual matters. We can find traces of rationalism in the works of St. Thomas Aquinas. He was a genius who saw its weakness and therefore rejected some of his intellectual work before he died.

At the end of the course on the paranormal, the lecturer sensitively approached me and asked if I would like to join the centre. She felt that I knew what she was lecturing about from the very beginning, and that I had the necessary ability to progress quickly in their organization. I politely thanked her and declined the offer.

On Monday I reported to Dr. Leherusie that the course was interesting, but its substance was not new to me. I have never asked for my special guide spirit because all my life I have prayed to my guardian angel as my parents taught me.

To illustrate what I mean about sensitivity to the paranormal, I offer another story. When Vera and I were living in Mississauga, once a month I would visit my friend's hermitage on a farm in the Peterborough area. One Sunday afternoon, I was tired and sitting in solitude in the hermitage. I put my head into my palms and closed my eyes. My mind was caught between being awake and sleep. I heard a fast repeating "tch-tch-tch" sound coming from several sources. It made me fully alert. *What is this?* I asked myself.

"These are the hearts of the wild geese flying over the hermitage," came the answer.

"What nonsense," my rational mind replied. "I am going crazy!"

"Not so," the first voice said. "Get out and have a look."

I stepped out of the hermitage and there it was—about thirty wild geese flying over the hermitage, landing on the pond near the hermitage. Strange! Unusual, isn't it?

About three weeks after the Spiritism course, I had a vivid dream. A young man dressed in blue appeared to me and told me his name. He said he was my servant and that I could call on his name whenever I had any difficulties.

I replied politely and reverently. "Thank you! I appreciate your willingness to be helpful, but I didn't ask for your help. Please, leave me alone."

"No," he said, "I want to serve you."

"No thank you," I repeated.

I woke up from the dream with his strange, two syllable name going through my mind like a mantra. I tried to stop it, but I couldn't. I prayed and tried to focus my mind on other things, but I couldn't stop the name from sounding in my mind. After two days I thought I needed psychiatric help, but at the same time I was afraid that the psychiatrist, except for offering me some pills, would not be able to help me.

After three days, I was sick of the name. I steadily suppressed it. I did not stop praying to my God, the real universal God of Jesus Christ and His good spirits for help, for liberation from the obsession. When I went to bed in the evening, I had one more dream. The fellow came back and said that he wanted to give me his spirit.

"No," I said.

He ignored my refusal and put his mouth on my mouth, trying to breathe his breath into me. He tried very hard, and I resisted equally hard ... as hard as I could. I realized that I was dealing with evil. What kind of a servant would he be, trying to control me against my will? I could not resist any longer and was about to break down, fearful that he had gotten the best of me. However, his strength broke down a fraction of a second before my resisting strength failed. He did not manage to give me his spirit.

Immediately I started to breathe normally again. A third person then appeared in the dream. It was an old man who spoke to the young fellow who wanted to be my guide and servant. "I told you not to mess with this fellow." From that moment, the strange name of the young fellow was erased from my mind and the mantra stopped. As a mere curiosity, I tried to remember the name on several occasions, but I could not. Even today I cannot remember it.

Perhaps the woman witch lecturer threw a spell on me when I declined to become a member of her coven. I had the strength to resist the powerful young spirit-man because I was ordained an exorcist at the Lateran Basilica in Rome before I was ordained a priest. I do not know. I can only speculate.

What is happening to our rational modern society that is refusing to see beyond the end of its nose, beyond the material dimension of reality? Why do some university-educated, rational people become involved with witchcraft? What influence do the various invisible beings have on us?

Witchcraft is real and is blossoming among us. This story is only a sketch. There's no need to be scared of it or to see the devil's fingers in all negative happenings, but it's good to be aware of it. Emotional and mental illnesses rooted in biology and chemistry are real, but that's not the whole story. Chemistry and electricity are not the only help in hopeless situations.

57. Durham, Ontario

DURING OUR MARRIAGE, VERA AND I SHARED MANY wilderness adventures, such as camping, canoeing and portaging. As we aged, our trips from Toronto and Mississauga north to Muskoka, Killarney and other places started to be too much for us in the heavy weekend traffic. We loved the wilderness. I dreamed about getting out of the large cities where I had spent many years and settling in the country, but that was not possible because of our careers. When Vera retired at the age of sixty, realizing my dream of moving to the country was possible: gushing rivers, lakes, forest, open skies, wild animals and white winters with fresh air.

To attain my dream, it was necessary to enter another job competition and find employment as a probation and parole officer somewhere north of Toronto. Vera stopped working, so it was up to me to keep our household financially afloat. I resigned my staff training position and became a probation and parole officer again.

Professor Josef Svoboda accompanied me on my search for suitable property. At the north edge of the town of Durham, on top of a hill, was a dilapidated farm house. The property bordered on a conservation area on the Saugeen River. There were waterfalls and a lake situated in a large recreational camping area. A probation and parole position was available in Walkerton, about thirty kilometers west of Durham. Lady luck was on my side again.

In Durham, Vera and I built our modest three-bedroom house with a basement room. The windows looked out onto the surrounding lush landscape. On the lower part of our property, hidden in the bushy area, we built our hermitage.

Vera became an organist at the St. Peter and St. Paul Catholic church. With her social skills and her sense of humour, we soon had many friends who would meet regularly at our house. We thought that this was it ... that we would live in Durham for the rest of our lives. My heart's desire was fulfilled.

One year after settling in Durham, a second heart attack landed me in the hospital in Hanover. There I developed a relationship with a young doctor, Bob Basilij. Nine years later he saved my life after successful quadruple by-pass heart surgery at University Hospital in London, Ontario. As a result of a doctor neglecting some of his responsibilities immediately after my surgery, I was poisoned. Ten days after my release from University Hospital, I was dying. Dr. Basilij did everything in his power to save my life. After my release from the General Hospital in Hanover, he kept prompting me to relocate from the beautiful but humid Georgian Bay area to the dry, clean air of the Colorado Mountains because of my heart condition. Vera refused to move to the United States saying, "In snow I was born and in snow I want to die." As I write these lines, her body lies under a thick blanket of snow in the Cranbrook Roman Catholic cemetery.

58. Cranbrook, British Columbia

WE LEFT DURHAM AFTER ELEVEN YEARS AND arrived in Cranbrook, British Columbia on a hot July day in 1994. Driving the rented truck down the main strip lined by motels, restaurants and gas stations, Vera remarked, "This is Cranbrook? It's like any American city—business, business, business. No life but business. I understand it, but I am disappointed."

Before we arrived in Cranbrook in beautiful British Columbia, I learned from a friend in Vancouver that Cranbrook had two Roman Catholic parishes, and that one of them had an open-minded, progressive and dynamic community. Christ the Servant was to be our new parish. The community accepted us with open arms and we fit in easily. Vera was in her element again. People around her with smiling faces! We were impressed with their welcome. On Saturday evenings and on Sundays, the church was packed.

With the help of two students, we unloaded our belongings into a two-bedroom apartment with a balcony on the top floor. This was to be our temporary home because I wanted to buy something better, but Vera resisted; she was content and did not see any reason for moving again.

The Marywood Retreat House, hidden among the surrounding forests and facing the peaks of the Rocky Mountains, was alive. It was operated by the ecumenically oriented Sisters of Notre Dame. We started to feel at home almost immediately. The retreat house was a bonus that we didn't have in Durham. On its property, I improvised a small hermitage using a camping trailer. Natural hot springs and ski hills were easily accessible by car. It became clear to us that we had not made a mistake. The mountain air was clean and dry, just as Dr. Basilij had recommended.

I cannot help but wonder what has changed during the past eighteen years. Christ the Servant parish and St. Mary's, the other parish, are half empty today compared to when we arrived. The congregations consist mostly of older people now; the enthusiasm that followed Vatican II somehow evaporated.

When I reflect on significant events during our years in Cranbrook, I do not recall many. Vera became a flower girl by taking care of the flower pots planted in front of Christ the Servant. She was an avid walker, walking the streets of Cranbrook and picking up garbage. She would remove the dying flowers from the decorative city boxes to make room for the young ones.

On two occasions we visited my siblings' families in the Czech and Slovak Republics. Vera regularly bought season tickets for the winter season of the Cranbrook Key

City Theatre. Listening to live music and watching stage plays were important to her.

In 2006, Vera was diagnosed with breast cancer and lost one breast. Her second breast followed two years later. She joked about it by saying that Dr. Aleem, her skillful surgeon, was a great collector of women's breasts. Vera admired and loved the kind man.

After the second surgery, Vera started to lose her energy, so we had to move to Joseph Creek Village retirement home. After almost two years there, we had to separate because I was no longer able to cope with Vera's dementia. I visited with her every day in her private room at Joseph Creek facility, except when I was seriously ill.

My prostate started to act up and I needed surgery. It was performed in Lethbridge, Alberta where I was kept in hospital for twelve days instead of two because of bleeding. For six months I had to wear diapers because of poor bladder control. Then Dr. Aleem, almost accidently by his touch during a medical examination, discovered that I had a dangerous aorta aneurism that required surgery.

Before I was rolled into the operating room, my anesthetist warned me about the possibility of dying on the operating table or having a stroke and being brain damaged. He asked whether I was still willing to go ahead with the operation. I replied that exposing myself to the possibility of dying was not new for me.

The operation was successful, except for one artery that did not close as expected. That led to another more complicated surgery two years later ... and to many CAT scans.

I survived it all, but kept getting weaker and weaker. Meanwhile, macular degeneration began in my eyes. My right eye is almost useless now. For a while my drivers' license was suspended, but I got it back after I passed a medical examination focused on my vision. Similarly, my hearing is getting worse. No longer can I drive lengthy distances because I am falling asleep behind the wheel. Recently I started to have sharp pains in my right leg, my groin and my back. Occasionally they require morphine. Doctors do not want to operate on me anymore.

The abdication of my clerical status still causes pain. It has prevented me from functioning formally as a priest in the Roman Catholic Church. The fact that God knows the truth, along with a handful of friends, is good enough for me.

I wish the Roman Catholic Church would become more catholic, that is broader and more ecumenical, more embracing, and more loving than its traditional and current emphasis on being Roman. I do not question the necessity of Canon Law or of the authority of the pope and the bishops. Just as Vera used to say, "In snow I was born and in snow I wish to die," I am saying, "As a baby I was baptized in the Roman Catholic Church, to that Church I have been faithful, and in the Roman Catholic Church I wish to die."

I do understand the ultra-conservative Roman Catholics who had a strong influence on Pope Benedict XVI. Their main motivation is attachment, their "love of wine in the old skins,"[12] and their fear of the new wine that inevitably will break all skins that are too old.[13] What about the words of Jesus Christ, when He said "Do not fear"?[14] I loved the liturgy in Latin. It is sweet and beautiful. For three years I was a master of ceremony in the seminary. I still could celebrate the Tridentine rite of the holy mass with my back towards the congregation, but I won't do it—I cannot do it.

My old guiding principle is "nova et vetera," that is, not only old traditional things, but also new things as modern sciences and psychological insights reveal them. Yes, reveal them! They are revelations that must be taken into consideration. Revelation is at the centre of Christianity.

To be a missionary in our modern, changing world, one needs to have experience and know that world, just as St. Peter was at home in the synagogues in the Diaspora or St. Paul in the Greek culture. We need mature priestly vocations coming from the world—married or unmarried. Of course, it would be more difficult to prepare them in the seminaries for the traditional priesthood. They would be more difficult to mold. What I am suggesting here is very easy to say, but difficult to accomplish. It would require a gradual restructuring of the canon law, an undertaking for which most of our clergy is not ready.

I love metaphors. They speak more forcefully and sometimes more clearly than sophisticated analyses, arguments and explanatory doctrinal systems. Unfortunately, metaphors don't speak to everybody. The disciples of Jesus often had a hard time understanding them.

I perceive the church as a big ship on the stormy waters of religious, economic, moral, and political history. The captain of the huge ship must be very careful, wise, and experienced—a born leader like St. Peter. The ship needs sails or engines that propel it, but it also needs a ballast to keep it steady. Depending on the sails and engines without the proper ballast will cause the ship to perish. Similarly, depending only on its ballast, the ship would stop, move backwards as pushed by the waves and eventually sink.

The beauty and attractiveness of the conservatism in the church represents the ballast. Progressive and searching Christian souls represent the sails or engines that move the ship forward. I believe that it is possible to grow in holiness, in humility and in love whether one is part of the ballast or part of the energizing sails.

JIŘÍ (GEORGE) HOŘÁK

VIII. EPILOGUE

"THE INTUITIVE MIND IS A SACRED GIFT AND THE rational mind is a faithful servant. We created a society that honors the servant and has forgotten the gift." This quote has been attributed to Albert Einstein; however, some have disputed this claim. Regardless of the source of this quote, it succinctly expresses my understanding of the human mind.

The intuitive level of the human mind is the superior dimension of mind where insights, ideas, creative feelings, and true happiness or darkness live, and where destructive behaviour originates. It's where our sense of beauty and enthusiasm live, but also where fear and horror reside ... if we allow it. For some people, inner impulses originate there in the form of voices.

It is the analytical and logical level of our mind where the intuitive insights, suggestions and impulses must be sorted out with the help of analysis, logic and rational principles, as it is done in research and technology. Without logical structures, confusion and unhealthy uncertainty and even illness, may follow. Eventually, psychiatric treatment may become necessary. Unhealthy emotional processes sometimes begin in a mother's womb and in early childhood. They may drain much of our energy and affect not only mental, but also physical health. They can also begin and develop later in life. In religious terms, we call them sinful.

These stories are a selection of my life experiences. The intuitive mind played an important role in them when they were developing. The stories were written in the spirit of transparency and in a reporting style. The names of the people in the stories are real, except for three or four instances when I intentionally changed the name.

If the reader considers my stories as fabrication or creative writing, as did my professor in the sociology course at York University, then I say that my life story is only one of many equally and more interesting life stories. To the disbelieving but thinking and reflecting reader, I suggest reserving judgment for twenty minutes, assume that these stories are true and then question the meaning of it all.

I am aware how tricky our ego becomes when it is repressed and its mischievousness is not recognized.

Without prayer, some of my anxious situations could have led to a sad end. Authentic Christian prayer is characterized by humility and love, concern for others, and turning one's focus beyond oneself to the Other, to God, to look in the same direction as the living, loving and creating God. It is not the monistic prayer of the New Age in which the individual gradually comes to believe that he/she is God.

With a smile, I am taking refuge in prayer right now while I type these lines. I am doing so not so much with words, as with my heart.

Jiří (George)

George Horak boating on Moyie Lake

George and Vera Horak 1969

George's first mass at St. Peter's Basilica 1958

George practicing yoga

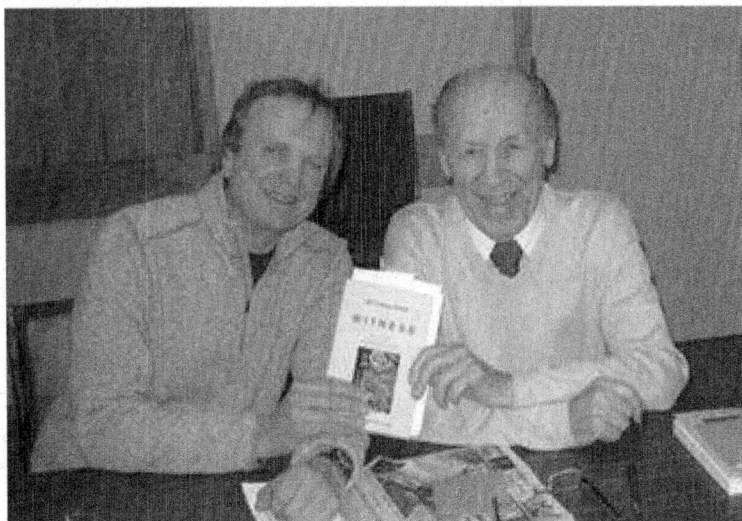

*Douglas Francis Mitchell and George
Horak at book signing*

X. NOTES

1. Leoš was a younger brother of Bishop Felix Maria Davídek.

2. Father Nesrovnal was arrested by the communists, badly beaten and then "fell out of a running train." In other words, he was murdered. That's what I heard when I inquired about him in 1990. How much is true I do not know.

3. Years later I met the other Jiří Hořák (political activist) for whom the police were searching in the USA. He was older than I.

4. Trochta was a Salesian. He was eventually sentenced by Communist jurisprudence to twenty-five years in prison for being an enemy of the people; before he died, he was elevated by Pope Paul VI to a Cardinal.

5. I met Father Pitrun later on in the fall of the same year in Salzburg, Austria. In 1958, he was my assistant priest at the Basilica of St. Peter in Vatican City, where I celebrated my first Holy Mass at the altar of St. Wenceslaus.

6. Alois Štěpán died in Chicago many years later. I never lost respect for him as an honest and courageous man with a beautiful, strong character. He was a wholehearted Christian.

7. I have learned from unreliable sources that shortly after the war in Italy, 240 priests were murdered by having their throats cut. It was done by special brigades.

8. For more information see http://www.madonna-house.org/

9. Antoine de Saint-Exupery, *Airman's Odyssey* (New York: Mariner Books, 1984).

10. Meditate seriously about the words "Thy will be done" in Jesus' Our Father prayer: Asking God to lead me; teach me that my will moves in the same direction as His loving creative will. In other words, that His and my will form a union in which we look no longer at each other, but know each other and look together in the same creative direction of life, truth and beauty and see ugliness and rebellion, as destruction and painful dying.

11. RCMP stands for the Royal Canadian Mountain Police. It is the Canadian federal police force.

12. Matthew 9:16–17; Mark 2:21; Luke 5:36.

13. Matthew 28:20.

14. Matthew 14:27.

CPSIA information can be obtained
at www.ICGtesting.com
Printed in the USA
LVOW03s1620040417
529578LV00004B/965/P

9 781460 295946